It Happened to Me

Series Editor: Arlene Hirschfelder

Books in the "It Happened to Me" series are designed for inquisitive teens digging for answers about certain illnesses, social issues, or lifestyle interests. Whether you are deep into your teen years or just entering them, these books are gold mines of up-to-date information, riveting teen views, and great visuals to help you figure out stuff. Besides special boxes highlighting singular facts, each book is enhanced with the latest reading list, websites, and an index. Perfect for browsing, there's loads of expert information by acclaimed writers to help parents, guardians, and librarians understand teen illness, tough situations, and lifestyle choices.

1. *Learning Disabilities: The Ultimate Teen Guide,* by Penny Hutchins Paquette and Cheryl Gerson Tuttle, 2002.
2. *Epilepsy: The Ultimate Teen Guide,* by Kathlyn Gay and Sean McGarrahan, 2002.
3. *Stress Relief: The Ultimate Teen Guide,* by Mark Powell, 2002.
4. *Making Sexual Decisions: The Ultimate Teen Guide,* by L. Kris Gowen, Ph.D., 2003.
5. *Asthma: The Ultimate Teen Guide,* by Penny Hutchins Paquette, 2003.

Sexual Decisions

The Ultimate Teen Guide

L. KRIS GOWEN, PH.D.

It Happened to Me, No. 4

The Scarecrow Press, Inc.
Lanham, Maryland • Toronto • Plymouth, UK

SCARECROW PRESS, INC.

Published in the United States of America
by Scarecrow Press, Inc.
A wholly owned subsidiary of
The Rowman & Littlefield Publishing Group, Inc.
4501 Forbes Boulevard, Suite 200, Lanham, Maryland 20706
www.scarecrowpress.com

Estover Road
Plymouth PL6 7PY
United Kingdom

Copyright © 2003 by L. Kris Gowen
First paperback edition 2007

British Library Cataloguing in Publication Information Available

Library of Congress Cataloging-in-Publication Data
The hardback edition of this book was previously cataloged by the Library of Congress as follows:

Gowen, L. Kris, 1968–
    Making sexual decisions : the ultimate teen guide / L. Kris Gowen.
        p. cm. — (It happened to me ; no. 4)
    Includes bibliographical references and index.
    ISBN 0-8108-4647-0 (alk. paper)
    1. Sex instruction for teenagers. 2. Sex. 3. Teenagers—Sexual
behavior. I. Title. II. Series
HQ35.G68 2003
306.7—dc21   2002151298

ISBN: 0-8108-4647-0(hardcover)
ISBN: 978-0-8108-5805-3 / 0-8108-5805-3 (paperback)

♾™ The paper used in this publication meets the minimum requirements of
American National Standard for Information Sciences—Permanence of
Paper for Printed Library Materials, ANSI/NISO Z39.48-1992.
Manufactured in the United States of America.

Contents

Acknowledgments   ix

Introduction   xi

  The Importance of Sex Education   xi
  What I Hope to Do in This Book   xiii
  Who Is This Person Anyway?   xv

1 Female Basics   1

  Reviewing Puberty   1
  The Hymen   2
  Menstrual Cycle—How It Really Works   4
  Discharges: A Normal Part of Being a Woman   7
  Irregular Periods   8
  PMS   10
  Going to the Gynecologist   11
  The Clitoris and Sexual Response (Orgasms)   12
  Breasts   14

2 Male Basics   17

  Reviewing Puberty   17
  Sperm   18
  Penises   19
  Testicular Cancer—Preying upon the Young   22
  Orgasms   25
  Pre-ejaculate   25

3 Pregnancy   27

  Getting Pregnant   27
  Think You Might Be Pregnant?   28
  Your Options   31
  Bringing Baby Home   43

Contents

4 Sexually Transmitted Diseases — 45

Who Gets STDs? — 45

First, the Basics — 46

Specific STDs—Recognize and React — 48

If I Don't See It, I Don't Have It, Right? — 56

Getting Tested for STDs — 57

Choose the Right Doctor for You — 58

Recent Research: Chlamydia in Teens — 59

Spread the News, Not the Disease — 59

5 Sex: What It Is, Who Is Doing It, What It's Like, and Other Important Questions — 61

Basic Stats on What Is Going on "Out There" — 61

How Do You Feel about Sex? — 62

What Is Sex? — 64

Are You Ready? — 67

The First Time — 68

6 Safer Sex — 75

What Is Safer Sex? — 75

Choosing to Not Have Sex — 75

What Is Sex? The Experts Answer the Question This Time — 76

Intimacy: Don't Knock It 'til You've Tried It — 79

Casual Sex — 82

Being Safe through Testing and Monogamy — 83

What Choice Are You Going to Make? — 86

The Safest Sex of All: Masturbation — 87

7 Birth Control Options — 93

Controlling Your Behavior: It's All up to You — 94

Barriers: Keeping the Sperm Away — 99

Hormonal Methods: Less "Fuss," Less Protection From STDs — 111

Surgery: Once It's Done, It's Done — 117

Emergency Contraception: The Morning-After Pill — 120

8 I Know What to Do, So Why Is It So Hard to
    Do What I Know Is Right?   121

Peer Pressure—From the Inside   121
Partner Pressure—Doing It to Stay Together   124
*Media Blitz—Don't the Movies or TV Talk
    about Anything Else?*   125
*Gender Pressure—Being a Boy or a Girl in a
    Sexual World*   129
Gender and Culture—Adding Fuel to the Fire   133
How Believing in the Names Prevents Safer Sex   134
*How the Heck Do I Think Differently from
    Everyone Else?*   135

9 Communicating about Sex   139

Know What You Believe   139
Know What You Want to Say   139
Know When Is a Good Time to Say It   140
Know How to Say It   141
Negotiating Strategies   144
Talking with Adults   146

10 Great Relationships   149

*Humans Need Relationships—But Not
    That Much*   149
Reasons to Like Someone   150
Crushes   152
*Now That We Are Together, How Do We
    Make It Last?*   155
Thinking about Your Relationship   157
Things That Can Make a Good Relationship Bad   158

11 Abusive Relationships   163

*Dating Violence and Abusive Relationships
    Are Everywhere*   163
Anyone Can Be a Victim   163
There Are Different Kinds of Dating Violence   164
The Warning Signs   166

Contents

How to Get Out of an Abusive Relationship   167
Where to Go   168
If the Abuse Is Taking Place in Your Family   168
Recovery Takes Time   169

12 Rape   171

What Is Rape?   171
Rape Drugs   174
What to Do If You Are Raped   175
Preventing Rape   178

13 Other Important Topics   181

Body Image   181
Older Guys, Younger Girls   183
Alternative Sexual Behaviors   185
Online Flirting and Dating   189
Breaking Up Is Hard to Do   192
Sexual Orientation   195
Interracial Dating   199
Drinking and Drugs and Sex   201

14 Conclusion   205

Notes   207

For Further Information   217

Index   223

About the Author   227

Acknowledgments

This book represents the ideas and experiences of many, in hopes of casting light on a hidden, complex, and emotional topic. Special thanks to Arlene Hirschfelder, Debra Schepp, Kim Tabor and Scarecrow Press for giving me the chance to write this book; Nancy Bateman for providing initial editorial feedback; Carolyn Laub and Donnovan Somera whose work at the Mid-Peninsula YWCA has affected many young lives in northern California; Molly McKenna for her pop culture knowledge and research expertise; Arttoday.com and the Library of Congress for illustration inspiration; Robert Brown for providing last-minute assistance on graphics; Nancy Brown and the doctors of the *We're Talking* teen health website, www.pamf.org/teen, for providing questions and answers for this book; and to my mother and father for their continued support and love. Without all of your work and dedication to this project, it would not be on the shelves today.

Introduction

THE IMPORTANCE OF SEX EDUCATION

I was happy and excited when I was asked to write this book. It was nothing short of a dream come true. Sex education (and other types of health education) is a main interest of mine—I've taught it, thought about it, and researched it quite a bit. Why? Because I think it's important.

Funny thing is, few people seem to think sex education is important. Look at the examples. At school, you don't spend a lot of time in sex ed classes, if you even have a sex ed class. Often, sex ed is taught during a biology class or a health class that doesn't even last the whole year. Subjects like math and English get more time and attention at every school in the United States. I'm not saying that math and English aren't important, but the amount of schooling you get in those two subjects as compared to sex ed is astounding.

Schools often don't spend a lot of time on sex education because administrators believe that sex should be taught in the home. Though, for the most part, not many parents want to talk about sex with their children—they want the schools to do it. And, to be honest, teens do not always want to hear about sex from their parents. (Your parents only had sex the same number of times as there are kids in your family, right?) So, your parents' idea of sex education may be something like:

"Wait until you're married."
"Don't get pregnant," or "Don't get someone pregnant."
"Use a condom please. I want you to be safe from AIDS."
And rarely is there actually any discussion involved.

Now, I do want to be fair. Some parents do a great job of talking to their children about sex. I mean really talking about it. They're open to questions, they listen to what you have to say, and they want to help. But they are sadly in the minority. And they should be applauded.

But for the most part, it comes down to this: Your school isn't giving you the answers you need. Some of them maybe, but not all for sure. And your parents are not letting you in on what they know about sex. So how important can sex education really be if no one is giving you the information you need? I mean, come on. Learning about sex *only* helps you learn about your body, your relationships with other people, and could possibly save your life. And are those things really *that* important?

Of course they are. But sex is a difficult subject to talk about—you know that. Sexual relationships are a very personal and private matter. And sex is also pretty abstract. The act itself is easy enough to describe, but all the emotions, feelings, and sensations that go along with it are not. So, talking openly about a personal, emotion-filled act is not an easy thing to do for anyone. It takes practice, time, and a lot of care.

So, what happens is that many teens end up with partial information about sex and sexual relationships. They collect bits and pieces from their classes, their parents' voices, and what they see on television and in the movies. Then, they try to fill in the rest of the information with what they hear from their friends, read on the Internet and in books, and of course, what they learn from personal experiences. And that's how most of us learn about sex.

It may not be totally accurate, but some information is better than none, right? Well, maybe. Some information is good, as long as that information is right. And, as we all

SINCE THERE'S BEEN SEX, THERE'S BEEN SEX EDUCATION

Historians believe that the first written document of sexual positions was written in China in 200 B.C. The better-known ancient sex manual, the *Kama Sutra,* was written in the third century A.D. The original *Kama Sutra* had 1,000 chapters—more modern versions of the book have been edited to "only" 150 chapters. This book was quite progressive for its time, stating that it was important for both "youth" and women to be educated in sex, and that all responsible citizens appreciate the importance of sex education.[1]

know, our friends, television, and other media are not always accurate. It is difficult to figure out what is and is not true sometimes. That is where I hope to come in—to help you figure out what is and isn't true in the world of sex and relationships.

WHAT I HOPE TO DO IN THIS BOOK

I am writing this book because I want to be a part of your sex education process. I want to help you fill in some of the blanks in your knowledge about sex and relationships. I also want to give you some things to think about when it comes to the feelings and emotions that surround sex. In short, I want to help you make your own decisions when it comes to relationships and being sexual with others.

This is a list of things I believe about sex education. I believe:

- ◎ **You have a right to ask questions and get the answers.**
- ◎ **You already know a lot, but not all there is to know, about sex and relationships.**
- ◎ **You're going to make your own decisions. Having access to information can only help you make those decisions the best way you can.**
- ◎ **No question should be left unanswered.**
- ◎ **After reading this book, you may make a different decision about the role sex plays in your life, or you may feel the same way about sex as you did before you read this.**
- ◎ **Asking questions doesn't mean you want to have sex right away.**
- ◎ **If you've already had sex, you still may have questions about it.**
- ◎ **You and only you can decide what is right for you.**

I promise to do my best to include information that I believe is relevant to your lives, and that may not have been given to you by others. I want to provide you with an education about sex that is practical, and gives you a sense of what is going on "out there"—in other people and the

worlds of research and politics—as well as inside yourself.
Yes, you'll already know some of the information in this
book. I expect most of you to know a lot of the
information here. But to tell the whole story, I need to
repeat some information that you may already know.

I will also do my best to remain nonjudgmental. I want
each and every one of you to make your own decisions
about what you do and do not want to do sexually. But, as
all humans do, I have opinions about these things. And
those may show through from time to time. Also,
sometimes I simply cannot help myself. I *do* think that there
is a "right" answer to some really difficult and
controversial issues. My opinions and answers developed
while doing research, teaching classes, and answering
questions in magazines and on the Internet about teens, sex,
and sexuality. And then there are my opinions formed
through my own experiences. But no matter what my
opinions are, I try to give both sides of every debate that I
bring up. And I'll provide resources for you to get more
information about each and every topic, so you can develop
your own beliefs about all the different issues. I believe it's
a great idea to learn what's on the other side of the coin, so
to speak. Looking at both sides of an issue can only serve
to strengthen your own opinions as you form them, and
maybe even change them as you learn more and more.

Not everyone is alike. We all have different experiences
that shape our beliefs and you have a right to feel what you
feel. You may find yourself disagreeing with what I have to
say, and that is more than fine—it is great to have your
own opinions. I do promise, however, that the facts in this
book are real, even if they are surrounded by opinions that
you simply do not believe. I hope what you'll learn from
reading this book, no matter what you believe, is that a
decision based on facts and serious thought is not only
better for you, it can also help shape who you are and who
you want to eventually become. In other words, as
important as the decision you make is, what can be equally
important is how you made the decision. Thinking about
why you do what you do is extremely important. It helps

you avoid making mistakes that could cost you future options or even your life.

It takes tremendous courage and strength to make a good sexual decision. Anyone can make a bad choice, or choose to do something without thinking about it. All sexual decisions and explorations are personal and need to be made for yourself first, and then your partner.

WHO IS THIS PERSON ANYWAY?

A fair question to ask is "Who is writing this book?" My name is Kris Gowen (the "L" stands for Laura, my first name, but I always go by Kris, and Dr. Kris). I have a doctorate in adolescent development from Stanford University. This means that by the time I graduated from everything, I was technically in the 21st grade. On some level, I was insane to do all that, but overall I really liked being in school for all those years. There were times when I thought I wasn't going to make it, and I took time off from school and worked in between my different degrees (something I highly suggest for any of you interested in graduate school), but overall I have no regrets being in school for that long.

While at Stanford, I did a lot of research on girls' body image as they go through puberty and sex education in schools. I wrote papers on how race and ethnicity relate to body image in girls, how body image relates to dating, and how one's family styles influence teen romantic relationships. I helped evaluate an AIDS Prevention Program that was taught by the local YWCA. I have also run online message boards and advice columns where teens can ask questions about sex and relationships. This has been my favorite thing to do. You will see some of the questions I got, along with my answers, in this book.

In graduate school, I helped teach an AIDS prevention program in high schools, and I taught a course on human sexuality to college students. After graduation, I lectured at the Stanford School of Education, where I taught teachers how to teach sex education (say that ten times fast), and I also taught them how to reach out to any of their students they felt needed a bit of support. A word about all those teachers—you may not believe it, but they care an awful lot about you. They worry and want to help. If ever you feel that you need an adult to talk to, and your parents are not an option, think of talking to a teacher.

When I am not dealing with anything related to sex education, I am either hanging out with my friends or doing something related to hockey. I have been an in-line goalie for several years, and love both playing and watching hockey. I also love to sing.

Thanks for taking the time to read the introduction. I hope that it gives you a basic idea as to who I am and where this book may take you. In short, what I hope to do here is provide honest answers to honest questions about sex and relationships. If you read this book and come away with new knowledge, or just end up feeling more comfortable about making sexual decisions, then I've done my job.

Happy reading!

Female Basics

REVIEWING PUBERTY

For girls, puberty usually begins between the ages of nine
and thirteen years and lasts about two or three years. The
first sign of puberty is usually the beginning of
breast development, followed by the growth of a
few pubic hairs. By midpuberty a girl continues
to grow breasts as well as pubic, leg, and
underarm hair, but she doesn't get her first
menstrual period yet. Her first period doesn't
usually happen until one or two years after the
first signs of puberty. First, inside a girl's body,
the vagina, ovaries, and uterus grow and many
girls get a clear or white discharge from their
vagina. Then, she'll experience menses, or her
first period. During midpuberty, a girl also goes
through her "growth spurt," during which she gets both
taller and heavier. It is extremely important to know that
it is 100 percent normal for a girl to gain
twenty-four pounds of fat during the two or
three years of puberty.[1] In fact, during puberty,
a girl's body fat content rises from about 8
percent to about 25 percent. This increase in
the amount of fat on her body is needed to help
it get ready to have a baby.

The start of the period is usually the signal
that a girl has entered late puberty. A girl's
clitoris grows larger as do her vaginal "lips,"
or labia. Her pubic hair also gets coarser and
grows a lot more. During this time, she continues to grow
a bit taller and larger, and her breasts finish developing.

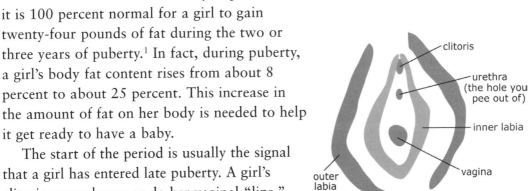

EATING DISORDERS AND PUBERTY

Because a girl gains a lot of weight during puberty, this is a common time for girls to become concerned about their weight, begin dieting for the first time, and possibly even develop an eating disorder. The earlier a girl enters puberty, the more likely she is to develop an eating disorder and become depressed.[2] This is because she feels very different from her friends and also does not like the idea that she is getting bigger when she knows that being skinny is associated with being pretty and popular. It is important to know that gaining a lot of weight during puberty is a normal and healthy thing to happen to the female body. Attempts to stop puberty by starving oneself can lead to serious health problems later in life.

THE HYMEN

The vagina is partially covered by a thin membrane (like a piece of skin) called the hymen. The hymen is also known as the "cherry" in slang terms. The hymen usually does not cover the entire vaginal opening, since there must be some way for the menstrual fluid, or period, to leave the body.

This membrane, although it has very little biological purpose, has great cultural significance. Some believe that the existence of an intact hymen on a woman means that she is still a virgin (and some women who talk about having sex for the first time will sometimes talk about having their "cherry popped"). However, many women who are virgins have their hymens either separated, torn, or stretched through exercise or using a tampon. Sometimes the hymen separates for no clear reason. Those who do not have their hymens torn prior to having sex for the first time may feel some pain and notice some bleeding the first time they have sex.

? Question:[3]
I was just wondering where that layer of skin, the hymen, is exactly. Is it right when you enter the vagina, or further in?
—Curious eighteen-year-old in Kentucky

Answer:
It is farther in, approximately one inch.
Sincerely,
Dr. X, *We're Talking* teen health website,
www.pamf.org/teen

? Question:
My boyfriend and I have been dating for five and a half years and recently we decided to start having sex. Once

during sex, my hymen broke all the way, so it is no longer a ring but now just two small separate pieces. Although they are not painful, they are uncomfortable because they kind of just "hang out" of my vagina. Is this normal and is there anything I can do about them?
—An eighteen-year-old in Virginia

Answer:
This does sound like a normal occurrence after the hymen breaks. In some, the remaining pieces of the broken hymen hang down, and in others they are not noticeable. After a few months this tissue will likely shrink and not bother you anymore. If it does bother you after a few months, you can have it removed, usually by a gynecologist.
Sincerely,
Dr. X, *We're Talking* teen health website

? **Question:**
Ever since I started my period I could never get a tampon in. It wouldn't go in at all, and I wasn't nervous. I tried every way possible. When my boyfriend fingered me his finger couldn't even get halfway in, it's like there's something blocking there. Then after a while of trying I get this terrible, hot, burning feeling in my vaginal area. It's a terrible pain. I then tried to get a tampon in after he fingered me and it went almost halfway in, and it didn't hurt, but there was no way to get it any further in there. What's wrong with me? I'm very afraid, this has been going on for years now.
—Seventeen-year-old female

Answer:
There is probably nothing wrong. If you haven't had sexual intercourse then your vaginal opening may be too small to accommodate a tampon. Digital manipulation (fingering) through sexual foreplay can stretch the hymen, the thin skin layer that partly covered the vaginal opening. Also have your doctor examine you to see if the hymen is fairly tight and needs some stretching, or even a small snip to widen it to accommodate a tampon. You can also go to

your doctor and ask her to help you insert a tampon.
Do not be embarrassed, she can help.
Hang in there,
Dr. X, *We're Talking* teen health website

MENSTRUAL CYCLE—HOW IT REALLY WORKS

Your period, your "time of month," your "friend"—
whatever you call it, most women experience menstruation
for the first time between the ages of nine and sixteen, and
every month (twenty-eight days or so) after that. The funny
thing is, although both girls and boys know about it, know
that it happens to females, the purpose of menstruation and
how it works remain a mystery to most people. This is a
sad thing. Knowing how the human body works allows us
to appreciate it that much more. Knowing how and why a
female menstruates allows people of both genders to unlock
the mystery of a woman's fertility cycle.

The bottom-line purpose of menstruation is so that a
woman can get pregnant. Each month, an egg is released
by one of a woman's two ovaries. The egg travels to the
uterus by way of the fallopian tubes. The idea here is that
once the egg is released, it will be fertilized by a sperm and
be on its way to becoming a fetus and ultimately a baby.
So, in order for the egg/future baby to be comfortable, the
uterus starts to develop a thick, cushy lining made up of
blood and nutrients while the egg is making its way down
the fallopian tube. In a way, the uterus is getting ready for
its "house guest"—one that it thinks will stay for about
nine months.

Most of the time, however, the egg is not fertilized and
just passes right through the uterus without even stopping
to say hello; it simply dissolves instead. Since the uterus
has no one staying in it, it doesn't need all that nutrient-
rich lining it created. So, it sheds this lining through the
vagina. It is this lining that is the blood of a woman's
period. This cycle of egg release and uterus preparation

will happen practically every month until the ovaries stop releasing eggs. Most women have their periods for about thirty years or more.

But, this description of the menstrual cycle is missing something important—the hormones! In fact, many people associate menstruation with a woman's hormones being totally out of whack. This is not the case. While it's true that women's hormone levels change with the menstrual cycle, they do so for very distinct reasons. These reasons are divided into three phases.

The Menstrual Phase
(day zero to day five, give or take)

The menstrual phase is basically the time you have your period. During this time, the endometrium (that cushy nutrient-filled lining built by the uterus) is shed, along with a little blood. Meanwhile, the body gets ready for the next egg to come along. Small pulses of gonadotropin-releasing hormone (GnRH) from the hypothalamus (a part of your brain) lead to small pulses of Leutinizing Hormone (LH) and Follicle Stimulating Hormone (FSH) from the pituitary gland. LH and FSH stimulate several follicles (each containing an egg cell) to develop in the ovaries. Only the strongest egg will survive this process and enter into the next phase.

The Follicular/Proliferative Phase
(about days six to fourteen)

Now, there is only one egg that has matured enough for eventual release—the survivor. The FSH continues promoting the growth of this egg and also tells a woman's body that it's time to increase the level of estrogen. This rise in estrogen acts as a signal for the uterus to start making its lining. The follicle (egg) continues to grow, getting itself ready for fertilization after release. When the level of estrogen peaks, that's the green light for the egg and off it goes on its journey.

Ovulation! The Time a Woman Is Fertile (day fourteen or fifteen, but really a woman can get pregnant for more days than just those two out of every month)

Estrogen is at its max point, and the follicle cage releases the egg. This process is known as ovulation. The ovum (one egg) then travels from the ovary down the fallopian tube and into the uterus. Now that the egg is released, the level of estrogen goes down, but not too much, as it still has to help build that lining in the uterus.

The Luteal/Secretory Phase (days sixteen to twenty-eight or so)

Once the ovum is released, the follicle it broke out of becomes a sac known as the corpus luteum. LH causes the corpus luteum to grow and to secrete progesterone, yet another female hormone. The progesterone makes the endometrial lining stronger, so that the uterus is ready for a baby. In a woman who doesn't become pregnant during ovulation, the level of progesterone peaks about a week after ovulation and then begins to drop along with the estrogen level. The flow of blood to the lining decreases, and at that point the lining breaks and sheds during menstruation. The dip in estrogen and progesterone at the end of the cycle helps let the body know that it's time to start the cycle all over again.

And that's how hormones get the female body ready to have a baby and deal with the fact that no baby is coming, should the egg not be fertilized. If an egg were to be fertilized during this time, that is, if a woman did become pregnant, the levels of estrogen and progesterone would stay high in order for the lining in the uterus to stay healthy and fresh. Because these hormone levels would not decrease, the menstrual cycle would not be signaled to start again. This is why pregnant women don't get their periods. There is no lining to shed—it's being used to feed the fetus inside her.

DISCHARGES: A NORMAL PART OF BEING A WOMAN

The word "discharge" often conjures up images of sexually transmitted diseases. Discharges are seen as unhealthy and unwanted. But, in reality, all women have discharges; discharges are simply fluids from the vagina that leave the body. An answer to a question about discharges by someone from the *We're Talking* teen health website talks about all the different discharges and what they might mean.

? Question:

What causes brown discharge? I haven't gotten my period in a while but recently I got a brown discharge. It only happened one day and hasn't since.
—Age sixteen female

Answer:

Vaginal discharge is normal and varies during your menstrual cycle. Before ovulation (the release of the egg), there is *a lot* of mucous produced, up to thirty times more than after ovulation. It is also more watery and elastic during that phase of your cycle. You may want to wear panty liners during that time. Discharges are abnormal only if they have a yellow or green color, are clumpy like cottage cheese, or have a bad odor. If you are worried, see a doctor.

Here are some descriptions of different discharges:

White: Thick, white discharge but small quantity is common at the beginning and end of your cycle. White discharge like cottage cheese and itchy often indicates a yeast infection. This can be treated by over-the-counter yeast vaginal creams or suppositories.

Clear and stretchy: This is "fertile" mucous and means you are ovulating.

THE HISTORY OF PROTECTION

Women have been using products to help control menstrual flow for almost all of history. The first references to tampons have been found in hieroglyphics—the writing of ancient Egypt—as early as 1550 B.C.! The first commercial tampons in the United States weren't sold until the early 1930s, however. Before tampons, most women used cloth napkins to absorb blood and then started to buy disposable pads. Although disposable pads were available in Europe as early as the 1890s, it was not until the 1920s that these were available in the United States.[4]

Clear and watery: This occurs at different times of your cycle and can be particularly heavy after exercising.

Yellow or Green: May indicate an infection, especially in a large amount or if it has a foul odor.

Brown: May happen right after periods, and is just "cleaning out" your vagina. Old blood looks brown.

Spotting Blood/Brown Discharge: This may occur when you are ovulating/midcycle. But if your period is late or scanty, pregnancy is possible. Check a first-morning urine sample for pregnancy.

IRREGULAR PERIODS

Now that we spent all that time talking about the menstrual cycle, it is important that you should know that more often a girl's menstrual cycle is irregular than regular. In other words, it is a lot more common for a girl to get her period at unexpected times than at expected times. Things like stress, diet, not getting enough sleep, and a crazy schedule can all make a girl's period start and stop at strange times. Read these questions and answers to learn more.

?

Question:
I started my period about two years ago and I still do not have it regularly. I skip several months before having one. It had been a long time (five to six) months since my last one. I don't feel comfortable talking to my mom and I don't have a regular doctor. Is this normal? What should I do? Is there a pill/vitamin I can take to have a period every month?
—Age seventeen female

Answer:
You don't mention if you are sexually active or not. If you are sexually active and haven't had your period for five or six months, you need to check a pregnancy test right away. If you haven't been sexually active, it is not that uncommon to still have irregular periods at your age. One option for

girls with irregular periods is to start on birth control pills. In this case, the pill is not used for birth control (unless you are also sexually active) but for regulating the timing of your period. It might be easier to tell your mom that you want a "checkup" rather than to tell her exactly what your symptoms are. You should make an appointment with a primary care provider (a family practitioner or general internist) or with an obstetrician/gynecologist for a checkup and to discuss your concerns.

Signed,

Dr. X, *We're Talking* teen health website

? Question:

I just got spotting today, and thought my period is starting, but all afternoon it's just been spotting! I don't know if it's staying or leaving??? Also, my cycle has changed! I usually get my periods at the end of the month, but today is April 4!! I'm not sexually active, so I know I'm not pregnant. What is this?? I'm confused??? Please answer back. Thanks.
—Age eighteen female

Answer:

It is very common for women especially young women to have intermenstrual spotting and occasional change in their menstrual cycle from normal. This can happen in relation to emotional stress or depression, increased exercise, fasting or dieting, and sometimes from a missed ovulation cycle (i.e., ovulation does not take place) and so the hormonal cycle gets disrupted. You should not worry, this sometimes resolves after one or two cycles. If, however, you start having persistent intermenstrual spotting or a persistent irregularity in your menstrual cycle then you should come in for an evaluation.

Signed,

Dr. X, *We're Talking* teen health website

Sports and Periods

You may have heard that many girls do not get their periods when they are seriously involved in athletics.

Almost any female who is in serious training for any sport is at risk for developing secondary amenorrhea, which is the medical term for the stopping of the monthly period after you used to have it for a while. Many things can cause secondary amenorrhea in female athletes—stress, a low percentage of body fat, and rapid weight loss are some of the culprits. Studies show that the more active and vigorous the sport, the more likely a female will have irregular, if not absent, periods.[5]

What's interesting is that scientists and doctors have mixed opinions as to whether experiencing secondary amenorrhea is dangerous or not—some think that not getting her period for a while puts a young woman at risk for osteoporosis (a bone-thinning disease).[6] Also, it's not clear whether girls who don't get their periods for a long time will get them again on their own once their athletic training is less intense.

CHECK IT OUT!

There is a whole Website dedicated to the history of menstruation, www.mum.org. Check out what women used to use as tampons throughout history, read about religion and menstruation, or learn about getting your period from a Kotex instruction booklet from 1938! Even get some great jokes about a woman's "little friend." It is all here.

For now, it's recommended that if you do not get your period for three months in a row, talk to a doctor about it to look for possible causes and solutions.

PMS

The changes in hormones that are responsible for menstruation can also cause women to experience emotional and physical changes during their cycle. The medical term for these changes is "premenstrual syndrome," or PMS. PMS was first recognized as a medical condition in 1931, but historical descriptions of the emotional and physical changes that go along with a woman's menstrual cycle have been discovered to reach as far back as Hippocrates' writings from the fifth century B.C.[7]

Almost 80 percent of menstruating women experience some form of PMS, although the symptoms and their intensity vary tremendously from person to person. Some women get very moody in an angry way, others in a sad way. Some women get very tender breasts, others get super-awful cramps. No one woman has the same type of PMS. Researchers believe that 20 percent to 40 percent of women who have PMS experience symptoms that make life difficult; another 2.5 percent to 5 percent report that their PMS takes over their lives.[8]

No one is exactly sure what causes PMS, but medical experts believe it's caused by a combination of things—physiological, genetic, nutritional, and behavioral reasons are likely to all be involved. There are, however, many ways to help someone feel better when they have PMS. Exercising can really help, as can other forms of stress reduction. Eating less refined sugar and cutting out caffeine and alcohol can also help reduce the symptoms of PMS. Finally, over-the-counter drugs such as ibuprofen are also effective.

GOING TO THE GYNECOLOGIST

Even though it is important for an individual to take care of her own sexual health, she can't do it all alone. There is a type of doctor that specializes in the female reproductive system. This doctor is known as a gynecologist—going to one once a year can keep you healthy and possibly prevent any potential problems from getting worse (or developing in the first place). A young woman should go to the gynecologist for any of the following reasons:

- **She is sexually active**
- **She is thinking of becoming sexually active**
- **She thinks she might be pregnant**
- **She turns eighteen**
- **She wants birth control that requires a prescription (the pill, diaphragm, cervical cap, Norplant, Depo-Provera)**
- **She experiences pain in her pelvic region**
- **She has an unusual discharge or bleeding from her vagina**
- **She has not had her period for six months (even though she has not had sex)**

What to Expect at the Gynecologist

Despite the stories you may hear, going to the gynecologist is not that bad. And knowing what to expect before you go can make the experience that much easier. A routine exam consists of several parts:

1. **Getting the Facts. You will be asked to fill out a form or answer questions about your overall health, your sexual experiences, and any medications you take. Be honest. All the information you give is confidential, and telling the truth will give your doctor the right information she needs.**

2. **A Breast Examination. Although you are most likely a bit young to be concerned with breast cancer, a gynecologist will most likely massage your breasts to look for any unusual lumps. Hopefully, she will also teach you how to do this yourself so that you can tell your doctor if you feel anything out of the ordinary.**

3. **Pelvic Examination. Your doctor will check out the outside of your vagina—the lips, clitoris, and all that. Then, she will use a speculum made of plastic or metal to open up your vagina and take a look inside. She will take a sample of your cervical mucus using a cotton swab (Q-Tip) or something that looks like a Popsicle stick. This may feel a little uncomfortable (the stretching and all), but it should not hurt. *Ask your doctor for a mirror so that you can look inside your body and see what she sees.***

4. **Bimanual Examination. Your doctor may insert a finger into your anus while she puts fingers from her other hand into your vagina. She does this in order to see if your ovaries and uterus are shaped okay.**

Stay healthy and go to the doctor!

THE CLITORIS AND SEXUAL RESPONSE (ORGASMS)

The clitoris is a small, sensitive organ whose sole purpose is to provide sexual pleasure. It's located right above the vagina and can look like a small button or knob. The clitoris often "hides" underneath a fold of skin called the clitoral hood. The clitoris, like the penis on a male, contains erectile tissue so that when a woman gets sexually excited, the clitoris becomes engorged (filled) with blood and becomes twice the size as it is in its more relaxed state.

Orgasms are the peak of sexual excitement and consist of a tensing and releasing of muscles in a series of contractions. Sometimes these muscle contractions happen all through a woman's body, while sometimes the muscle contractions are more focused in the vagina or groin area. Most women have an orgasm as a result of having their clitoris stimulated, but some women have orgasms through sexual intercourse. There is absolutely nothing wrong with a girl if she can only have an orgasm through masturbation or manual stimulation by her partner. Because so much attention is focused on having sexual intercourse, and not necessarily on sexual pleasure and stimulation, only one out of every four girls has orgasms with any regularity.

There is no one way for a girl to have an orgasm, but there are some things that are pretty necessary. First, the girl needs to be comfortable with herself and her partner (unless she is masturbating, then she is her own partner!). She also needs to feel relaxed and comfortable with where she is. Her clitoris most likely needs stimulation, and interruption of this stimulation can prevent a girl from having an orgasm. Finally, the most important thing is that the girl is enjoying herself. That way, she is more likely to feel loved, sexy, and aroused.

It's really hard to describe what an orgasm feels like, as they feel different to different people, and they can even feel different to the same person in different situations. Some people feel them as a huge rush, while others feel more of a tickle, then a sense of relief. Some people feel them all over their body, while others feel them just around the genital area. Sometimes parts of the body go numb or feel like they are asleep. Some people make noise, some laugh, some stay quiet. Sexual expression is very different from person to person, and there is no right or wrong way to react.

There is a lot of hype around the female orgasm, and it's hard to sort out the truth. Researchers try, but many things remain a mystery, or a myth. For example, the jury is still out when it comes to female ejaculation—some people say it exists, while others do not. Same thing goes with the

"G-spot." There are some women who swear by this special, extra sensitive area inside the vagina, and others who think it's a load of baloney. And then there is the issue between the clitoral and vaginal orgasm; some people try to say that one is better than the other, but the truth is an orgasm is an orgasm. The female body has more nerve endings in the clitoris than in the vagina, so that's why some women have an easier time or can only have an orgasm if their clitoris is stimulated. But it's important to remember that so much of sexual attraction and responses come from how a person feels. Therefore, whether a person orgasms or not has just as much to do with how that person is feeling emotionally as it does with what that person is experiencing physically. The more relaxed, happy, confident, and comfortable a person is, the more likely an orgasm will be a part of her sexual activity.

KNOW THYSELF, EXAMINE THYSELF

Unlike males, females can have a hard time understanding their reproductive anatomy simply because they cannot see it as well as a male can see his. However, it's important for a woman to get to know her body, and there is nothing shameful about taking a look "down there" to see what it's all about. To see your vulva (the name for all the external parts of the female reproductive system), sit with your legs apart and use a mirror. You might have to separate the labia (lips) to see the whole picture, but it's well worth it. By becoming familiar with what your body looks like when it's healthy, you are better able to realize if something doesn't look right, and be able to tell your doctor about it.

BREASTS

Breasts are relatively simple parts of the female body, made up of milk (mammary) glands and ducts, connective tissue, and fat. They start growing around age eight or nine and finish growing by age seventeen or eighteen. Breasts do not have any muscles; no matter what exercises a person performs, they will not get any bigger. Creams, pills, and other products don't work either. The only way to increase the size of a breast is to gain weight; more fat means more breast.

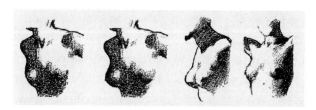

All women have breasts at some point (some women have theirs removed as a result of a mastectomy), and most women complain about their own. They feel their breasts are either too big, too small, too lopsided. They believe their nipples are too brown, too small, too pointy. The truth is, there are as many types of breasts as there are women; no two pairs of breasts are alike, and for that matter, no two breasts are alike. What I mean is that no one has completely symmetrical breasts, especially younger women; for some reason, the two breasts on one person will sometimes grow at different rates, and thus a person will look lopsided until their breasts are done growing. Even after full maturity, however, all women's natural breasts are lopsided and many adult women will have breasts different enough in size that it's noticeable (but really, people tend to not look that closely). Same thing goes for nipples. Nipples come in all different sizes and shapes, and no one has the same nipples as anyone else.

Why does our society care about breasts so much? Really, all they're there for is to be a source of food for an infant. But as you all know, the significance of breasts as a sexual part of a woman's body gives them a whole new status among body parts. They are stared at, gawked at, and sometimes touched. Breasts, especially the nipples, can actually be a very sensitive and erotic place on a woman's body—nipples will often get hard and erect from any sort of stimulation, such as touch and cold weather. This is because the nipple is made of erectile tissue, just like a penis. But not all women like to have their breasts touched during intimate moments. And NO women like their breasts touched by some random person who for whatever reason thinks they have the right to do it. If someone touches another person's breasts without permission, especially in a public place (like a concert, or school hallway), that person has committed a form of sexual assault. This action is not to be taken lightly. Breasts are unique in that they are a sexual body part that can be seen through clothing. But just because anyone can see them does not mean that anyone can touch them.

Male Basics

REVIEWING PUBERTY

For boys, puberty usually begins between the ages of nine and fourteen years and lasts several years. The first sign of puberty is usually when the testes (balls) start to grow, the scrotum (the wrinkled skin that holds the testes) turns darker, and a boy starts to get hair on his body. By midpuberty pubic hair can be seen, and his penis starts to get larger (more on this later). Body odor may become a problem as his armpit sweat glands become active. Then comes the growth spurt where a boy can grow up to four inches in just one year; a boy's body will also become more muscular. Increases in testosterone, which also are responsible for muscle development, cause the boy's voice to crack, then deepen to an adult male pitch.

A common occurrence during puberty is the "wet dream." As the testes begin to make sperm, and other parts of the

Male Anatomy: Inside and Out

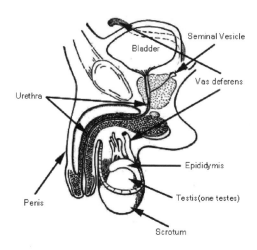

By Andrew Klink, inspired by arttoday.com

body create the ejaculatory fluid ("cum"), semen is produced for the first time in the male. In fact, semen production is highest in the early stages of puberty because hormone levels are highest during this period in a man's life (this is also why a boy will have many erections during this time). Since semen is constantly being made, it needs to be released from the body at some point. So, unless a boy masturbates to release the semen, the build up of semen will release itself on its own at night during nocturnal emissions, or "wet dreams."

SPERM

Sperm, the male's contribution to baby making (in the same way that a woman provides the egg), are made in the testes (also known as "balls"). The testes hang away from the body because in order for the sperm to develop properly, they must stay at a slightly lower temperature (95° to 97° Fahrenheit, 35° to 36° Celsius) than normal body temperature (98.6° F, 37° C).

Once the sperm are made, they have to travel from each testis to a coiled tube on the outer surface of each testis called the epididymis, where they mature in around three weeks. Sperm exit the body through the penis during ejaculation. When the penis is stimulated, it becomes erect, and ejaculation propels mature sperm from the epididymis through a long tube (vas deferens or ductus deferens) inside the body. While the sperm is traveling through the body, it gets mixed with nutrient-rich fluids from the seminal vesicles and a milky secretion from the prostate gland. The sperm and fluids together are known as semen, or cum.

Semen does three things:[1]

⑨ **Provides a watery environment in which the sperm cells can swim while outside the body,**

⑨ **Provides nutrients for the sperm cells,**

⑨ **Protects the sperm cells by neutralizing acids in the female's sexual tract.**

Thanks to all the fluids in the semen, the sperm can leave the penis in a protected environment full of nutrients and acid-fighting materials so that it has a better chance of surviving and making its way into the female body and fertilizing an egg.

PENISES

Of all the concerns a boy has in his life, worrying about penis size tends to keep him awake at night the most. And this concern does not go away as a boy gets older; grown men also spend much too much time worrying about something they can do nothing about. While it is true that not all penises are the same size, they are generally between three and a half to four and a half inches when soft and five to seven inches when erect. A smaller penis will increase in size more than a larger penis when becoming erect, so those concerned about a smaller soft penis can rest assured that when erect, it makes up ground.

You've heard it before, and you will hear it again here: size does not matter when it comes to how many orgasms one can have, how fertile someone is, or how well a person can satisfy his partner sexually. Communication, a good relationship, and true care for your partner make for a good sexual relationship. The size of your penis will not matter if you truly care about your partner and are interested in having a healthy sexual relationship.

CIRCUMCISION

Circumcision is the surgical removal of the foreskin on the penis. On an uncircumcised male, the foreskin covers the glans, or the tip, of the penis. On a circumcised male, the glans is exposed. Circumcision usually is performed on infants for religious or cultural reasons but can be done on older males for health reasons. Some believe that it's better to remove the foreskin in order to avoid infections; however, as long as an uncircumcised male washes his penis and underneath his foreskin, infections should not be a problem. Circumcision does NOT decrease the risk of penile cancer as once thought. About 70 percent of males are circumcised in the United States at birth, but this percentage is decreasing over the years as people learn it's not a necessary medical procedure.[2]

Questions about Penises

There are a lot of questions boys (and some girls) have when it comes to penises. Here are some to help you think about what is normal and perhaps not-so-normal when it comes to this part of the body. If you at any time believe that something might be wrong with you, do yourself a favor and ask a doctor about it. It is better to be safe than sorry!

? Question:[3]

Why do some guys have penises that look different? Some have skin that cover the head of their penis and others do not. Is there a health reason for this or is it because some just want to be different? I saw one with a bunch of skin and it was strange looking."
—Curious

Answer:

Great question! A penis with skin on it has not been circumcised. When a boy is a baby, many parents circumcise them—this means that they remove the skin that covers the head of the penis (this skin is called the foreskin). If a baby is not circumcised, then he will have extra skin on his penis, like the one you saw.

People circumcise their babies for religious reasons and for health reasons. Some people think that being circumcised makes it easier to keep the penis clean and prevents it from getting infected. But as long as the boy washes his penis and makes sure he washes under the foreskin, he is okay.
Dr. Kris[4]

? Question:

I know that a bent penis is very common but my problem is that it seems to be crooked. When I get an erection it isn't straight but rather points more to one side—not that it is perpendicular to my leg but still. I don't think it has always been like this but I'm not positive. Is this normal? I'm not having sex right now but will it complicate sexual intercourse? Could masturbation be the cause of this? Is there any way to straighten it out?
—Seventeen-year-old male

Answer:

Penis sizes vary considerably and many men have a penis that bends to one side or another or "stands straight up" when erect. It will not matter at all—sex is about relationships and intimacy—pleasing a partner includes many things not related to penis size (or crookedness)—and the quality of the interaction can be measured by how well you learn what makes your partner feel good, emotionally and physically.

Try not to worry,

Dr. X, *We're Talking* teen health website

? Question:

My penis has become "numb," I think from excessive masturbation. It is now harder for me to get sexually aroused and up to this summer I was masturbating at least once each day. How can I heal the "numbness"?

—Sixteen-year-old male

Answer:

You really can't cause numbness from "excessive masturbation." "Excessive" really only has to do with the effect masturbation and the preoccupation with sex have on the other facets of your life (in other words, does it interfere with you developing social relationships or interfere with you getting your work done?). However, if you masturbate or have sex too frequently, it can make your urge to have sex less intense, and the sensations that you experience less pleasurable. If you masturbate less frequently, the sensations may improve.

Good Luck,

Dr. X, *We're Talking* teen health website

? Question:

I was wondering does the amount of testosterone in your body affect penis growth? I have heard that more testosterone in the body shrinks the penis. Is that true?

—Seventeen-year-old male

Answer:

Testosterone is necessary to cause the penis to develop and to grow normally. Having too much testosterone is very rare, but it does not cause any problems with growth and development of the penis.

Good Luck,

Dr. X, *We're Talking* teen health website

? Question:
I am uncircumcised and it hurts to touch the head of my penis sometimes. Could there be something wrong?
—Eighteen-year-old male

Answer:
The head of the penis is sensitive in everybody. Masturbating can certainly cause it to be sensitive, especially if it is done without any lubricant (such as a water soluble lubricant like KY jelly). As long as the foreskin can be pulled back to allow the head of the penis to be cleaned, the foreskin is not a problem. It is important to pull the foreskin back down, covering the head of the penis after it is cleaned.
Good Luck,
Dr. X, *We're Talking* teen health website

TESTICULAR CANCER—PREYING UPON THE YOUNG

Cancer of the testicles accounts for only about 1 percent of all cancers in men. BUT, it is the most common type of cancer in males aged fifteen to thirty-five. The good news is that testicular cancer is curable 90 percent of the time if it's found early.[5] And, not only is it curable, but most testicular cancers are found by men themselves, either as a painless lump, a hardening or change in size of the testicle, or pain in the testicle. So, as a male, you have control over when your testicular cancer is found and treated! All you have to do is conduct the testicular self-exam once a month.

What Is a Testicular Self-Exam (TSE)?

The TSE is a method for boys and men to check their testicles to make sure there aren't any unusual bumps or lumps, which may be the first sign of testicular cancer. Sometimes cancer of the testicles will spread, so it is important to detect it early so that the cancer doesn't become more serious.

How Do I Do a TSE?

- Check yourself right after a hot shower, when the skin of the scrotum is relaxed and soft.
- Become familiar with the normal size, shape, and weight of your testicles.
- Using both hands, gently roll each testicle between your fingers.
- Find the epididymis. This is a ropelike structure on the top and back of each testicle. This structure is NOT an abnormal lump.
- Be on the alert for a tiny lump under the skin, in front or along the sides of either testicle. A lump may feel like a piece of uncooked rice or a small cooked pea.
- Report any swelling to your health care provider.

If you have any lumps or swelling in your testes, it doesn't necessarily mean you have cancer, but you should be checked by your health care provider.

Here are some other symptoms that may hint that you might have testicular cancer:

- A lump in either testicle, ranging in size from a pea to a golf ball;
- Any enlargement or swelling of a testicle;
- A significant shrinking of a testicle;
- A change in the hardness of a testicle;
- A feeling of heaviness in the scrotum;
- A dull ache in the lower abdomen or in the groin;
- A sudden collection of fluid in the scrotum;
- Pain or discomfort in a testicle or in the scrotum.[6]

If you have some of these symptoms, talk to your doctor as soon as possible. If detected and treated early, testicular cancer is one of the most curable cancers. Having testicular cancer doesn't necessarily mean that you will have one of your balls removed, and you will most likely be able to have children later in life. So, if you are at all concerned about testicular cancer, talk to your doctor about it!

AM I AT RISK FOR TESTICULAR CANCER?

At present, no one really knows what causes testicular cancer. We do know that it's not contagious, so you can't get it from someone else. There are some risk factors though. These include:

- Uncorrected undescended testicles in infants and young children (parents should see that their infant boys are checked at birth for the undescended testicles);
- A family history of testicular cancer;
- An identical twin with testicular cancer;
- An injury to the scrotum.[7]

A SURVIVAL STORY

At age twenty-five, Lance Armstrong[8] was a world-class cyclist, winning the World Championships, the Tour Du Pont, and multiple Tour de France stages. At age twenty-five, Lance Armstrong was diagnosed with testicular cancer. He had many of the warning signs, but chose to ignore them—he didn't have time to see a doctor, as his bike racing took priority. By the time he was diagnosed, the cancer had spread to Lance's abdomen, lungs, and brain. Despite the late diagnosis, Lance underwent aggressive treatment and beat the disease. He educated himself about testicular cancer and did everything he could to help himself get better. Since his diagnosis and treatment, Lance has won the Tour de France four years in a row, from 1999–2002! Today, he has a foundation dedicated to help people manage and survive cancer. Check out the Lance Armstrong Foundation at www.laf.org.

ORGASMS

Just like females, males also experience orgasms as the peak of their sexual excitement. And, also like females, orgasms consist of a tensing and releasing of muscles in a series of contractions. In fact, when random people are asked to write down what an orgasm feels like to them, it's hard for other people to tell whether a male or female wrote the description; in other words, the plumbing may be different, but the feelings are similar.

But there are differences between male and female orgasms. Male orgasms are usually more obvious than female ones because they happen when a guy ejaculates, or cums. Also, unlike in females, males experience what is called a refractory period right after they have an orgasm. This is a time of "recovery" for the male body where it becomes physically impossible for a guy to have an erection immediately after having an orgasm. Females don't experience this refractory period, which is why some females are able to have multiple orgasms, while males can't.

PRE-EJACULATE

Pre-ejaculate (also known as pre-cum) is that little bit of lubricant that you may notice at the tip of an erect penis before ejaculation happens. This fluid helps protect the sperm against the acids in the urethra (caused by urine) and also gives the sperm an extra slippery boost upon ejaculation. It's important to know that pre-ejaculate can have sperm in it, as well as any STD bacteria or virus. Therefore, it's not a good idea to let an erect penis get near another person's openings where they are vulnerable to getting an STD or pregnant.

TOO MUCH OF A GOOD THING?

?

Question:
Is it normal for your testicles to be sore after ejaculating a bunch of times in a short period of time, say three to five times in a day or two?
—Nineteen-year-old male

Answer:
Yes, it's normal. When a man ejaculates, his pelvic muscles and the muscles which move the testicles up and down have very strong contractions. These muscles may tend to ache if one ejaculates too frequently. It's not dangerous, it just hurts.
Good Luck,
Dr. X, *We're Talking* teen health website

Pregnancy

3

GETTING PREGNANT

There is only one way for a pregnancy to happen—a sperm from a male has to fertilize an egg from a female. Due to the wonders of science, this phenomenon can happen outside of the female body. However, for this book we are only concerned about pregnancies that happen during penis–vagina intercourse.

A female can only get pregnant during certain times of the month, when she is ovulating. Ovulation occurs about once every four weeks, when the ovaries release an egg. If a sperm happens to be inside a female when the egg is released (or is still alive inside the female when the egg is released), there is a high chance that a pregnancy will happen. There are 180 million sperm in a single ejaculation. It takes only one to make a girl pregnant.

There are many people out there who believe that as long as a couple has sex when a girl is not ovulating, then there is no chance of pregnancy. While this is true in theory, there are many problems with this line of thinking. First of all, it's very difficult to predict when a female will ovulate— she can even ovulate during her period! This is especially true for young females, whose periods have not been occurring long enough to establish a regular pattern. Remember from chapter 1—stress, diet, travel, and other things can all prevent a menstrual cycle from being regular. Now think about the average teen—her periods have only been around for a few years, and there are a lot of stress and diet changes in her life. And if that teen is in college, you can often add frequent travel to the mix. Predicting a young female's menstrual cycle becomes almost impossible,

First by a long shot:
Number of teens who give birth each year in different countries[1]

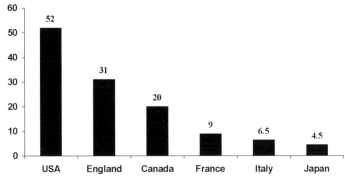

and thus knowing when she can and cannot become pregnant is an equally challenging task. Then you also need to consider the lifetime of the male sperm. Sperm can stay alive in a female's body for up to six days. So, even if you know when a girl is going to ovulate, you don't know how long the guy's sperm will live inside her body. This makes trying to figure out what days are "safe" to have sex even more difficult. There are classes where couples can learn how to predict when having sex will get the female pregnant, and when it will not. It takes one to two years to go through these classes, which are run by a trained professional.

If it takes one year of careful instruction to learn how to predict ovulation, trying to figure out how to do it on your own doesn't sound like such a good idea. There are many different birth control methods available to you, and using one is a much better idea than trying to guess when it is and is not safe to have sex in order to avoid pregnancy.

THINK YOU MIGHT BE PREGNANT?

If you think you could be pregnant, it's very important to find out sooner rather than later. The earlier you find out, the more options you have. First of all, finding out that you aren't pregnant will probably decrease your stress level and you can get on with your life. Finding out that you are pregnant early in the pregnancy either allows you the option of an abortion or early prenatal (before birth) care.

The first three months of a pregnancy are an important time for the fetus, and getting good prenatal care is essential for both mom and baby-to-be during this time. So do yourself and your baby a favor; get a pregnancy test pronto if you think you're pregnant!

There are a few signs of early pregnancy. The most obvious one is missing a period. If you miss a period, don't panic yet; missing periods is common in young women; just because you miss a period doesn't automatically mean you're pregnant. (Some young women wait to see if they miss two periods before getting a pregnancy test. The choice is yours.) But, if you have engaged in unprotected vaginal sex and you miss your period, look for these other signs of early pregnancy:

- Nausea/vomiting/feeling queasy (some people refer to this as "morning sickness" but the nausea can happen at any time of the day!);
- Soreness or enlargement of the breasts (don't confuse this with your breasts simply growing if you are of that age!);
- Increased need to urinate (because the fetus is pressing on your bladder);
- Feeling faint or tired;
- Just "feeling" pregnant.

RECENT RESEARCH: TEENS AT RISK FOR BIRTH COMPLICATIONS

Teenagers who give birth are at greater risk for developing complications than older women. Because teens are still growing and going through many changes related to the reproductive system, their babies are more likely to be born prematurely and have a higher chance of dying at birth. If a teen mother has a second baby, there is even a greater risk of birth complications, and there is a higher chance that the baby will be a stillborn (in other words, born dead).[2]

There are two ways you can get a pregnancy test, through a clinic or by taking a home pregnancy test. It's probably best to go to a clinic. There you can make sure that the test is accurate and medical professionals are around to talk to you about the results of the test whether they are positive or negative. These people aren't as nervous as you might be and will make sure that everything is done exactly right. Most home pregnancy tests available today are very accurate (97 percent), but only if you follow the instructions on the box exactly as they are written! Studies

⊚ ⊚ ⊚ ⊚ ⊚ ⊚ ⊚ ⊚ ⊚ ⊚ ⊚ ⊚ ⊚ ⊚ ⊚ ⊚ ⊚ ⊚

TEEN PREGNANCY—KNOW THE FACTS

Here are some basic facts about teen pregnancy in the United States.[3]

▶ Each year, almost 1 million teenage women—10 percent of all women aged fifteen to nineteen (that is one out of every ten) become pregnant. That means for every five teen women that has sex that year, one will become pregnant.

▶ Half of all first teen pregnancies happen within the first six months following first intercourse, and 20 percent happen within the first month.

▶ Most teen pregnancies—78 to 85 percent—are unplanned. These unplanned teen pregnancies make up about one-fourth of all accidental pregnancies annually.

▶ More than half (56 percent) of teen pregnancies end in birth, while 30 percent end in abortion, and the other 14 percent end in a miscarriage.

▶ Teen pregnancy rates are much higher in the United States than in many other developed countries—twice as high as in England and Wales or Canada, and nine times as high as in the Netherlands or Japan.

▶ One in fifteen men father a child while they are a teenager.

▶ The partners of teen moms tend to be older; about one in five babies born to teens under eighteen years old are fathered by men five or more years older than the mother.

▶ Teen moms have a good chance of having more than one baby while still young—one-fourth of teen moms have a second child within two years of their first.

show that some pregnancy tests can be very confusing so that the results are read correctly less than half the time (that is, people are more likely to read the results incorrectly than correctly!)—so it may be best to be tested by a professional to make absolutely sure you know if you are pregnant or not.[4]

Pregnancy tests work by measuring a hormone the body starts producing after the fertilized egg begins to grow. For that reason, it's important to wait at least two weeks after you have sex in order for an accurate pregnancy test. Waiting these two weeks gives your body a chance to create enough hormone to cause the test to turn positive; take the test too early and you'll get a result that says you aren't pregnant when you might very well be. Pregnancy tests, whether taken at the clinic or at home, work by measuring the amount of this hormone in your urine (pee). It's best to take a urine sample from your first bathroom trip of the morning. This is because urine is most concentrated in the morning, as you have not had anything to drink all night while you were asleep. The more concentrated the urine, the more likely you'll get an accurate test.

YOUR OPTIONS

Mistakes happen. Whether or not birth control is used, if a couple has penis–vagina sex, there's a chance that pregnancy can occur. Obviously, the more precautions a couple takes, the less chance of pregnancy. But, there are exceptions to every rule. If you find yourself involved in an unplanned pregnancy, here are your legal options for what to do next.

Abortion

You've heard it all from both sides. Abortion is murder. Abortion is a woman's right to choose. Abortion is a sin. Abortion is safer than giving birth to a child. Depending on your point of view, all of these statements can be true. But, no matter who you are, this statement is always true: *Having an abortion is not easy. Ending a pregnancy in this way will be emotionally difficult. You will remember this event for the rest of your life.*

Now, this doesn't mean that having an abortion is the wrong decision for you. It may be the right one; in your eyes it may be the only one; about half of all teen pregnancies end in abortion. Legally, only the woman has a right to choose an abortion. The man in the relationship has no legal right in the decision-making process. It would be nice if the two people who created the pregnancy could sit down together and talk about options, but there's nothing in the law that states that this must happen. It's the woman's body, so it's ultimately the woman's decision.

However, a woman under eighteen who is pregnant may not be able to legally make a decision about abortion on her own. The laws about abortion vary from state to state as to whether or not she needs to get permission from her parents (or a guardian, or relative) to have an abortion. Actually, the state laws differ quite a bit, ranging from needing no permission or notification (in other words, parents do not even need to know that their child is getting an abortion), to needing full consent from both parents for the abortion. You can find out about the laws in your state by calling a health clinic in your area, or by calling Planned Parenthood.

There are some of you out there who think that your parents would throw you out of the house or physically hurt you if you were to tell them that you were pregnant and thinking about getting an abortion. I'm not talking about many of you who think "Oh my God, if my mom found out, she would kill me," upon receiving a bad grade on a report card, or breaking a fine china plate while dusting. I'm referring to those of you out there who honestly would fear for your safety if your parents found out you were pregnant and wanted an abortion. For you, there is a way to get an abortion without getting their permission, no matter what state you live in, no matter what the law says. Through a process called "judicial bypass," a young woman can go to court and get the state's permission for an abortion. This is not an easy process, but for some it's the only option. A health clinic will help you understand the law better if you decide that this is something you need to look into.

The History of Abortion

Abortion laws have changed constantly throughout American history. Here is a very brief timeline of the major events that have influenced this issue.[5]

Before 1820: Abortion was legal in the United States
1820: Abortions after four months of pregnancy became illegal
By 1900: Most abortions were outlawed

1965: All abortions were outlawed

1973: The Supreme Court, under the *Roe v. Wade* decision, declared abortion legal because of our constitutional right to privacy

1976: The Supreme Court, under the *Planned Parenthood of Central Missouri v. Danforth*, declared it unconstitutional to demand a husband's permission if his wife wanted an abortion

1977: Through a series of decisions, the Supreme Court declared that public (in other words, government) funds did not have to be used to help pay for abortions

1992: The Supreme Court decided, in *Planned Parenthood of Southern Pennsylvania v. Casey*, that a state could require antiabortion materials to be distributed in clinics before a woman had an abortion and that a woman would have to return to the clinic twenty-four hours later in order to actually have the abortion

2000: In *Hill v. Colorado*, the Supreme Court declared that abortion protesters had to provide a 100-foot buffer zone around abortion clinics so that patients could have access to its doors.

Currently, abortion remains legal in the United States for all women. However, minors (those under eighteen years old) may need parental consent before having an abortion. There are many debates in the government concerning abortion still under way including banning late-term abortions (sometimes called "partial-birth" abortions), the use of genetic material from aborted fetuses for disease research, and trying to make all abortions illegal.

**THINK ABOUT IT:
WHY IT MIGHT BE A GOOD
IDEA TO TELL YOUR PARENTS**

You may not want to tell a parent about an unintended pregnancy, but here are some reasons why it may be best to talk about it in the long run:

▶ Having an abortion is an intense experience. Hiding it from them could be very difficult;

▶ You could use their support. Sure, they might be upset at first, but parents have a perspective that younger people often do not have;

▶ Abortions are expensive—several hundred dollars—and many insurance plans cover them. Talking to your parents may get you the financial help you need;

▶ You might need a ride, help making an appointment, or the name of a trusted doctor;

▶ You could use a shoulder to cry on.

IN THE NEWS: LEGAL BATTLES

Many states are now trying to decide whether to make parental consent necessary before any girl under eighteen has an abortion. While these debates are going on, most states are allowing teens to get abortions without parent permission; however, it is always best to call a clinic in advance to see what laws apply in your state.

In 2001, there was a bill about teen abortion laws that would have made it a federal misdemeanor for anyone other than a parent or guardian to take a girl to another state for an abortion. Although the bill was passed in the House of Representatives, it was defeated in the Senate. At the time of this writing, the bill is now dead, though legislatures often bring it up for debate. Stay tuned!

What Happens during an Abortion?

There are a few different types of abortion. In this book, I only talk about the two simplest forms, as these are the most likely types you may encounter. As the pregnancy progresses, the riskier the abortion procedure becomes. Although I am not suggesting that you should hurry your decision to have an abortion, having one more than four months into a pregnancy is not advised. At that point, the baby is very developed, and both the laws and the medical procedures become more complex.

For pregnancies in the first trimester (up to twelve weeks), a procedure called suction-aspiration is performed. The woman lies on her back, with her feet in stirrups like in a gynecological exam. Then, the cervix is numbed and stretched using smooth metal rods. Finally, a suction machine is inserted into the uterus, which pulls the fetus and placenta out. Although the procedure takes less than fifteen minutes, the whole appointment will last two to five hours total because of the paperwork, questions, laboratory tests (to make sure you really are pregnant), medications, anesthesia, procedure, recovery, and aftercare that's needed.

For pregnancies that are slightly further along (twelve to twenty-four weeks), the Dilation and Evacuation (D&E) procedure is performed. Although the actual procedure takes about thirty minutes, a woman has to go to the clinic the day before the abortion to prepare for the procedure, so really the entire process takes two days. During the preparation on the first day, the doctor will dilate (enlarge) the cervix (opening of the uterus), by inserting a small rod or series of rods into the cervix. Overnight these rods gently expand, opening the entrance to the uterus. The next day, the woman goes back to the clinic for the abortion. During the abortion, the woman is put under general anesthesia, which means she is "put under" while this is happening. The doctor uses a suction device to remove the fetus, and may also use a curettage (an instrument used for scraping) to help remove the fetus. The woman will remain at the clinic for one to several hours to make sure everything is okay. If she is not bleeding heavily, or showing other signs of complications, she will be allowed to leave. Some women, however, are kept overnight.

The Deal with RU486

On September 28, 2000, the Federal Drug Administration (FDA) approved mifepristone, the clinical name for the French-developed abortion pill, known as RU486. This abortion method has been available in Europe for over ten years. RU486 works by preventing the actions of the hormone progesterone, consequently thinning the lining of the uterus so an embryo cannot remain implanted and grow. As a result, the embryo is expelled from the body through the vagina. This procedure is 92 to 95 percent effective and can be used during the first eight weeks of pregnancy. There is also a shot, called methotrexate, that can be taken instead of taking the mifepristone pills. The number of doctor visits required and how it works are pretty much the same.

Taking RU486 requires three visits to the doctor. During the first visit, you take three mifepristone pills. Two days later, you return to the doctor's office to take another drug, misoprostol, which causes the uterus to contract and expel the embryo (sometimes this medication is taken at home, but more than likely you will go back to the doctor to get it). Feeling nauseous and experiencing cramping are normal, but the doctor will tell you about possible side effects that signal any danger. Finally, you need to see the doctor two weeks later to make sure that the abortion is complete, and there are no serious complications.

Taking RU486 is the same as getting a surgical abortion, from a legal standpoint. That means, all the laws about teen abortions in your state will apply to taking RU486 too. For more information on RU486, and other abortion issues, visit www.naral.org.

Adoption

Some girls do not believe they are ready to be a mother, yet they also do not believe in an abortion, do not want an abortion, or cannot have an abortion. For these girls, giving their baby up for adoption is a possible solution to their pregnancy. However, it is very uncommon for teens to decide to give their babies up for adoption—only about 4 percent of pregnant teens choose this option.[6] It is not easy to decide to give up a baby for adoption, and it's important to remember that adoption is permanent. The baby that the girl carries inside her body for nine months will not be a part of her family once it is adopted by another family. Because adoption is permanent, it's important to think about why you're considering putting your baby up for adoption. If the reasons you list are temporary, then you might want to consider living through some tough times in order to keep this little person-to-be in your life. But, if the situations you are facing are more permanent, or you are absolutely certain that you cannot take care of a child any time soon, then considering adoption might be a good idea. But before you make your decision, make sure that you do not do it alone. Talking to your parents, a counselor, the father of the child and his family can help you see what support you may or may not have if you decide to keep the baby. A young mother cannot take care of her child by herself; she needs friends, family, and money. If you don't have these resources, taking care of a child is close to impossible.

HELPFUL HINT

Check that the counseling you seek is not antiabortion—people with an agenda can scare you into making a decision that you will later regret. Find someone with an open mind, someone who can help you consider *all* your legal options.

If you decide that you want to give up the baby for adoption, look up adoption in the yellow pages of your phone book. You'll see many choices—some are for-profit, some not-for-profit, and some even focus on specific religions and ethnicities. If it's important to you that the child has parents of the same racial and/or religious background as you, ask the adoption agency if they have parents of your background on their waiting list. Choose the adoption agency that you think is right for you, or call a few to see which you think is best (see below for a list of questions to ask about the adoption agency and the potential family of the baby).

There are two types of adoption: confidential and open. In a confidential adoption, the birth parents and the adoptive parents never know each other. The only information the adoptive parents have about their new baby is important medical information so that they can make sure their baby gets the best care possible. In open adoptions, the two sets of parents know something about each other. What they know can vary a lot. At a minimum, a birthmother can pick the adoptive parents by reading some profiles of parents and choosing the family she thinks is best. At the most, you will stay in contact with the adoptive parents as the child grows up. You can write, call, and even visit the baby and parents. At this time, only fifteen states have this type of adoption relationship available; call an adoption agency near you to see what types of open adoptions are available in your state. In 69 percent of adoption cases, the birth parents had met the adoptive couple.[7]

Putting a baby up for adoption is a legal procedure. Although the birthmother doesn't need to have an attorney, some girls choose to have one in case problems arise. However, most adoptions are handled by the attorney of the adoptive parents, or an adoption agency. The birthmother is required to sign papers that say she is voluntarily giving the baby up for adoption. Sometimes these papers are signed before the child is born, sometimes after. The father of the child must also sign similar papers, saying that he is consenting to the adoption. If the father denies his role in the pregnancy, he needs to sign papers that legally document his refusal to admit he's the father. If the birthfather cannot be found, the attorney or adoption agency must make a decent attempt to find him. If the birthmother is not sure who the father is among multiple people, she must get papers signed by all the possible fathers.

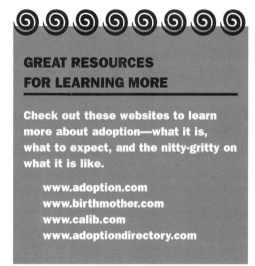

GREAT RESOURCES FOR LEARNING MORE

Check out these websites to learn more about adoption—what it is, what to expect, and the nitty-gritty on what it is like.

www.adoption.com
www.birthmother.com
www.calib.com
www.adoptiondirectory.com

Questions to Consider

Even once you decide to place the baby you are carrying up for adoption, you'll still have many questions to ask and answer yourself. Every time you meet with someone regarding the adoption, make a list of questions beforehand. Here are some questions that will help you get started. Feel free to add some of your own.

Questions to ask the adoption agency about the adoptive family:

How long has the couple been together?
Does the couple have children already?
Why is the couple looking to adopt?
What kind of life do they lead right now? What kind of recreation or hobbies do they enjoy?
What are the couple's values? Do they have strong religious beliefs?
How old are they?
Will both parents work or will one stay home with the baby?
What is the couple's view on disciplining a child?
Does the couple have extended families?
How do their families feel about adoption?

Here are some questions to ask yourself:

Do I care what religion the couple follows?
Do I care about the racial or ethnic backgrounds of the couple?

Do I want my child to have older brothers or sisters?

Do I want the couple to live near me?

Questions for potential parents:

Do you have any experience with children?

What do your families think about your adopting a baby?

Will you tell the child that he is adopted? When and how?

What will you tell the child about me? About his birthfather?

What are your religious beliefs?

What are your beliefs about education?

What forms of discipline will you use with the child?

Are you willing to maintain contact with me as your child grows up?

What type of contact are you most comfortable with?

How often would you like to stay in contact with me?

These questions have been provided and used with permission by www.birthmother.com, a great site—check it out!

Keeping the Baby

Being Pregnant

No two people experience pregnancy in the same way. Some will get a traditional case of "morning sickness," where they vomit every morning and feel awful. Others will get their "morning sickness" in the afternoon. Others will not get morning sickness at all. Same thing goes for food cravings—some women get them, some don't. Some women will get very moody while others will have a very calm emotional time. Don't worry about how you experience your pregnancy. As long as you go to a doctor on a regular basis for your prenatal care, and do what your doctor recommends, your baby and you will be as healthy as can be.

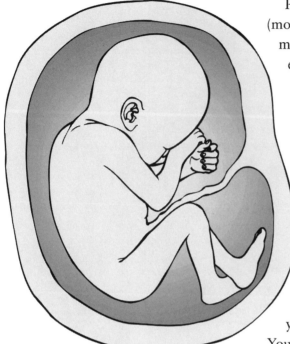

Pregnancies last about nine months (more like forty weeks if full term, but many young mothers have their babies earlier) and are divided into three trimesters, with each trimester lasting about three months. As each trimester passes, a pregnant woman experiences different sensations and feelings. Here are a few examples to give you an idea of what it's like to be pregnant.

First Trimester

You pee more often because the baby is starting to press against your bladder;

You might feel tired—a lot of your body's energy will go toward helping the baby grow;

You might feel nauseous at times;

Your period will get very light or stop;

MOVIE REVIEW

Mi Vida Loca: My Crazy Life (1993)
Latina gang girls Sad Girl and Mousie both fall in love with the same boy and each has a baby with him before they reach their sixteenth birthdays. Once best friends, they become bitter enemies in a quest for the father's attention.

MOVIE REVIEW

Riding in Cars with Boys (2001)
Drew Barrymore plays a brain who finds herself pregnant and married when she's fifteen years old. Sure, she overcomes the difficulties of being a teen mom, but not before she deals with issues of child neglect, a disapproving family, and other stresses.

Your may feel moody;
You don't look pregnant.

Second Trimester

You start to look pregnant;
Your abdomen hardens and expands;
You feel the baby move inside your womb;
You might notice a discharge coming out of your
    nipples;
You might get a dark tint to your face that will go away
    after the baby is born;
You might experience heartburn and hemorrhoids.

Third Trimester

Other people can see your baby move—it looks like
    ripples under your skin;
You might get backaches from the weight of the baby
    and you will probably walk differently because of
    your new body shape and weight;

You might start to feel "phantom contractions"—not the real thing, but a sort of practice your body goes through;

Your baby will be born.

The Delivery

The process of delivering a baby is called going through labor. Labor starts when a woman feels contractions and the baby shifts into place, getting ready for birth. During *early labor*, which can last several hours, there is little pain involved; the contractions will only last a minute or less. At the next stage of labor, sometimes called *active labor*, the contractions may or may not be longer, but they are only two minutes apart. A woman's emotions will be running at full speed—a woman going through labor can be easily irritated, so anything she says during this time should not be taken seriously. She might be angry at the world, her doctor, or her partner just because they are not going through the same experience as she is.

The *transition* is the most intense, and thankfully shortest, part of labor. A woman often makes a lot of noise, and may feel very cold. She will also get very thirsty. Some women want medication during this time, as they will be tired and in pain and feel as though they cannot go on. Some women prefer not to take any medication, despite feeling uncomfortable. The choice is up to her.

Next comes *stage II* of the delivery. This is when the baby is born. The woman has to push until the baby starts to go through the birth canal. Pushing can take up to two hours; the first time a woman has a baby is

TIPS FOR THE LABOR "COACH"

If you are a friend or partner of a woman having a baby and are there at the delivery, here are some pointers about your role:

- Assure the mother-to-be that she is not alone and you are there with her and for her;
- Make her feel as good as possible, both physically and emotionally;
- Help her communicate. You may understand what she is trying to say better than her doctor or nurse can;
- Let her squeeze your hand when she is in pain;
- Stay calm and happy. She will pick up on your mood.

usually the longest time she will have to push. Once the pushing is over, the baby is a part of the world.

The last part of delivery is the delivery of the placenta, the sack of nutrients that the baby had been living in for the past few months. It is normal for a woman to keep feeling contractions during this time.

BRINGING BABY HOME

The baby is born and you're now a parent. Right away you will feel tired—even if you were not the one who gave birth. Having a baby is an emotional experience and once the

delivery is over, the sense of relief washes over everyone and a feeling of utter exhaustion takes over. For the woman who actually had the baby, her fatigue is that much stronger; her body

went through a huge ordeal giving birth, and now her hormones are working hard to get back to normal. Her body is in overdrive. But even though a new parent is tired, there will not be much time for sleep. Babies do not sleep through the night, so neither will you.

The most important part of caring for your new baby is getting to know him or her. This time with your baby is known as bonding and is an important part of the child's development. Hold your baby. Put your finger in his or her hand and notice how the baby will grip it automatically. Talk to the baby even though he or she does not understand what you are saying. The baby will learn to recognize your voice as a sign of comfort and safety. Smile, laugh, and look at him or her. Don't be shy—the two of you are going to have a great life together. There is no experience in the world that can compare to that of being a parent. The challenges and frustrations will be great, but so will the rewards.

SAD, BUT TRUE

Children of young mothers are:

➤ More likely to be in poor health;
➤ More likely to have poor nutrition.[8]

Young mothers are:

➤ Less likely to finish their education;
➤ Less likely to find employment;
➤ More likely to be in poor housing;
➤ More likely to be socially isolated.[9]

THE BABY BLUES

As soon as a woman gives birth to a baby, her body will go through many changes to get it back to its original nonpregnant state. It is normal for a woman to feel sad and depressed for up to a week after her baby is born simply because of hormonal changes. But for a number of women, this time of depression lasts a lot longer and is much more serious. These women are victims of postpartum depression. They feel they cannot cope, believe they are horrible mothers, and are emotionally unstable. If you or someone you know is feeling this way, know there is help. Talk to a doctor or visit a site on postpartum depression such as the Pacific Post Partum Support Society at www.postpartum.org. The worst thing to do is ignore the situation when there is so much help out there.

4 Sexually Transmitted Diseases

WHO GETS STDs?

As we have already learned in chapter 3, about 800,000 teens in the United States get pregnant every year. And of those pregnancies, 85 percent are unwanted by the mother.[1] Thinking about your own life and the people you know, it would not be surprising if you know someone who was pregnant before the age of twenty or who is now a teen mom. Most teens know at least one person who has had this experience.

However, do you know at least one person who has a sexually transmitted disease (also called an STD)? If you say no, you are not alone—not many teens think they know someone who has a sexually transmitted disease. But, I will let you in on a little secret: More teens get a sexually transmitted disease than get pregnant every year. In fact, three million sexually transmitted diseases are contracted every year by teens[2]—more than three times as many as there are teen pregnancies. That means one in eight teens has an STD—one in four sexually active teens has an STD.

Why are there more cases of STDs than teen pregnancies every year? Here are a few reasons:

- Both boys and girls can get an STD; only girls can get pregnant.
- Girls can only get pregnant a few days out of the month. Anyone can get an STD, no matter what time of the month.
- There are many ways to get an STD. There is only one way to get pregnant (we are not talking about artificial insemination here, folks).

Given all these facts, here's a question to ask yourself: Why is it that even though more teens get STDs than get pregnant we know about the teen pregnancies in our school or social circle, but not the STD cases? Wouldn't it make sense that if there are three times as many STDs as pregnancies, we would know three times as many people with STD cases than with pregnancies? One would think, but there are reasons this is not the case:

- In public, you can tell if someone is pregnant after a few months. You cannot tell if people have an STD if you see them walking down the street;
- There are some people out there who brag about getting pregnant or getting someone pregnant. I have yet to meet someone who brags about getting, or giving someone, an STD;
- A person may turn to a friend if they are concerned about a pregnancy. They do not really turn to friends about concerns over STDs. At least, not as much;
- Many people do not even know they have an STD.

So, besides an unexpected pregnancy, sexually transmitted diseases are the thing teens (and adults, for that matter) want to avoid when they have sex. But unlike pregnancy, I have not known anyone who wants to get an STD. Sure, there are some teens out there who want to get pregnant, but I really do not think there is anyone out there who tries to get an STD. Knowing what the different STDs out there are, what they look like, and how to avoid them is an important part of anyone's sex education.

FIRST, THE BASICS

As the name "sexually transmitted disease" suggests, a person can get an STD from having sex with a person who is already infected with the disease. However, having sex with someone is not the only way to get an STD. Some STDs can be transmitted by sharing needles (which can happen during IV drug use, or while getting a tattoo), and some STDs such as critters (or "pests"), can be transmitted by simply sharing a towel with an infected person. However, sex is the main way STDs pass from one person to another. The trick is to realize that sex is not just a penis-in-vagina activity. Having anal sex or oral sex are also ways that STDs can be transmitted. In fact, herpes and gonorrhea are easily passed from one person to another through oral sex. Anal sex and oral sex are *not* safe behaviors. True, you cannot get someone pregnant those ways, but you (or someone else) can get sick or infected.

There are basically three types of STDs: critters, bacteria, and viruses. Critters are just what they sound like—little pests that live on or just underneath your skin. They look like tiny, tiny bugs, and sometimes you can actually see them with your own eyes if you look close enough. Although nasty sounding and unpleasant, critters are the easiest STDs to get rid of. All you have to do is wash yourself and all your belongings in really hot water using a special shampoo that you can get at your local pharmacist (read the label for specific directions). The two main types of critters are scabies and crabs. The bummer is that besides being easy to cure, they are easy to catch from another person. Although they are grouped under sexually transmitted diseases, you do not have to have sex with someone to actually get this disease. Sharing a bed or a towel with someone who has scabies or crabs is enough to get them—all these critters have to do is crawl from one warm body to the next.

The next type of STD are bacteria. The good thing about these STDs is that they can be cured—all you have to do is go to the doctor, take some antibiotics, and the disease is gone for good. The bad news is that these STDs often have no symptoms. You look fine, you feel fine, but you are not fine. It's only until months or years later that you realize something is wrong, and by then it may be too late to kill them with simple antibiotics. Long-term effects of untreated bacterial STDs include sterility (not being able to have children forever) and serious internal infections.

The last type of STD is the virus. This type of STD is the worst simply because there is no cure for any of them. Once you get a virus, it's yours to keep—and give to others—forever. The other superbad thing about some viral STDs is that they will eventually lead to death.

SPECIFIC STDs—RECOGNIZE AND REACT

Now that you know the basic categories of STDs, here are some descriptions of specific STDs that are pretty common among teens. If you see them on a partner, do not have sex with that person until he or she gets checked out and cured, if possible. If you see these symptoms on yourself, go to a doctor or health clinic as soon as you can to get the best possible treatment.

Chlamydia

Type: Bacteria

Symptoms: Approximately 75 percent of women and 50 percent of men have no symptoms. Those that do experience a watery discharge, painful urination, itching, and burning.

Treatment: When diagnosed, chlamydia is easily treated and cured with antibiotics. It's important to take all of the medication prescribed to cure chlamydia, even if the symptoms or signs stop before all the medication is gone. It's possible to get this STD more than one time in your life.

If Left Untreated: Up to 40 percent of women with untreated chlamydia will develop pelvic inflammatory disease (PID). Of those with PID, 20 percent will become infertile and 18 percent will experience intense, chronic, pelvic pain. Women with PID, if they get pregnant, have a 9 percent chance of having a life-threatening tubal pregnancy. In men, untreated chlamydia often results in a urethral infection (the urethra is the tube you pee out of), and may also result in swollen and tender testicles.

Gonorrhea

Type: Bacteria

Symptoms: In women, the early symptoms of gonorrhea are often mild, if there are any at all (up to 80 percent of women have no symptoms at all). Even when a woman has symptoms, they can be so general that the woman mistakes gonorrhea for a bladder or vaginal infection. The initial symptoms and signs in women include a painful or burning sensation when urinating and a vaginal discharge that is yellow or bloody. Only about 50 percent of men have some signs or symptoms, such as a burning sensation when urinating and a yellowish-white discharge from the penis. Sometimes men with gonorrhea get painful or swollen testicles. A person can also get gonorrhea in the anus (by having anal sex) or in the mouth (by having oral sex). Signs of an anal infection include discharge, anal itching, soreness, bleeding, and sometimes painful bowel movements. Infections in the throat cause few symptoms.

Treatment: When diagnosed, gonorrhea is easily treated and cured with antibiotics. It's important to take all of the medication prescribed to cure gonorrhea, even if the symptoms or signs stop before all the medication is gone. It's possible to get this STD more than one time in your life.

If Left Untreated: Women with untreated gonorrhea might develop pelvic inflammatory disease (PID). Of those with PID, 20 percent will become infertile and 18 percent will experience intense, chronic, pelvic pain. Women with PID, if they get pregnant, have a 9 percent chance of having a life-threatening tubal pregnancy (the fetus starts to grow in the fallopian tube—where there is no room for it—instead of the uterus). In men, gonorrhea can cause epididymitis, a painful condition of the testicles that can lead to infertility. Gonorrhea can also infect the prostate and can lead to scarring inside the urethra, making urination difficult.

Which are which? STDs by Type

Bacteria (curable)	Critters (curable)	Viruses (<u>not</u> curable)
Chlamydia	Pubic Lice	Hepatitis B
Gonorrhea	Scabies	Herpes
Syphilis		HPV (Genital Warts)
Trichomoniasis		HIV/AIDS

Hepatitis B

Type: Virus

Symptoms: Many of the symptoms are general, like poor appetite, vomiting, and headaches. The more unique symptom is jaundice, which is the yellowing of the eyes and skin.

Treatment: This is the only STD that has a vaccine—ask your doctor about it. Many people do eventually recover from Hepatitis B; however, they are not completely cured.

If Left Untreated: You can recover, but some people suffer serious liver damage or cancer.

Herpes Simplex Type II (Genital Herpes)

Type: Virus

Symptoms: Outbreaks of painful, bubbly blisters. The sores then open up and ooze or bleed, then finally scab up and go away (they will come back again later). The entire genital area may feel very tender or painful.

Treatment: Herpes can never be completely cured, but staying healthy can help decrease outbreaks. Certain pills can also help make the symptoms less severe and outbreaks less common. There are also ways to make the sores less painful, such as keeping them clean and dry.

If Left Untreated: The outbreaks will be more severe and happen more often. These outbreaks are usually most noticeable within the first year following the first episode. But once you have herpes, you always have herpes, and it can always be transmitted.

?

Question:[3]
I kissed someone that had kissed someone else that might possibly have herpes in the mouth.
Can I get it?
—Eighteen-year-old female

Answer:
Yes—it is possible. If you have ever had a cold sore in your entire life you may already have it. The Type 1 oral herpes virus is very common, most adults have already been infected in childhood. We recommend that people with active cold sores not kiss others, especially infants. Kissing a person who kissed a person is a bit far-fetched—but you can never say never with viral infections.
Sincerely,
Dr. X, *We're Talking* teen health website

HIV/AIDS

Many people do not realize that HIV and AIDS are two different things. Even though they are closely related to each other, they are not the same and it is important to know the difference between them. To put it simply, HIV stands for human immunodeficiency virus, the virus that causes AIDS. AIDS (acquired immune deficiency syndrome) is the end result of HIV infection. In other words, HIV is the virus that causes AIDS.

Now, here are the details about HIV:

Type: Virus
Symptoms: You cannot rely on symptoms to tell if you have HIV or not. Many people who have HIV do not show symptoms of the disease for many years. The only way to tell if you have HIV is to get tested. In the same way, you cannot tell if a person has AIDS by knowing the symptoms. The symptoms of AIDS are similar to the symptoms of many other diseases.
Treatment: There is no cure for HIV/AIDS. When someone tests HIV positive, they should live a very healthy lifestyle. It can be a serious matter to get sick if you are HIV positive or have AIDS. A person can

What are the chances?
Chance of getting an STD after having sex once with an infected person[4]

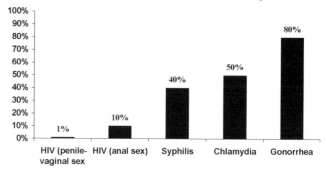

take medications (which are very expensive) to slow the progress of the disease.

If Left Untreated: AIDS is 100 percent fatal. Everyone who gets AIDS eventually dies from complications of the disease.

HPV (Genital Warts)

Type: Virus

Symptoms: Genital warts look like clusters of flesh-colored cauliflower bumps on your genitals. However, since these warts can pop up inside a woman's vagina, they may be hard to see on her. Genital warts are soft and usually itchy.

Treatment: Because genital warts are caused by a virus, they cannot be cured. However, there are chemicals that can burn them off of your body. Genital warts can also be frozen or cut off, or removed with a laser. However, there is a good chance that they will come back again (and again . . .).

If Left Untreated: There is a link between genital warts and cancers of the cervix, vagina, and penis. So, if you are diagnosed with genital warts, you are at a higher risk for developing one of these cancers later in your life.

? Question:

I have not been sexually active for more than eighteen months, but the other day two small, red bumps appeared on the shaft

of my penis. Could this just be a couple of pimples, or is there a chance that I could be showing symptoms of HPV even though I haven't had sex in over a year? Can I show the signs of genital warts this long after my last sexual encounter?
—Nineteen-year-old male

Answer:

It is hard to tell what the bumps might be without seeing them. As you may know, the only real way of diagnosing genital warts is by visual inspection. Don't hesitate to see your doc if they do not go away or if you are curious about what they may be. The ones you describe could indeed be just pimple type lesions. But without seeing them, it's a guess. Yes, it is possible to not show any signs of several sexually transmitted diseases for months or years before they finally express themselves. Condom use is strongly recommended, as is care of selecting a partner. Genital warts or HPV, in particular, can be avoided nicely by using a condom. Genital warts can have serious consequences for females, such as cervical cancer.

Best,

Dr. X, *We're Talking* teen health website

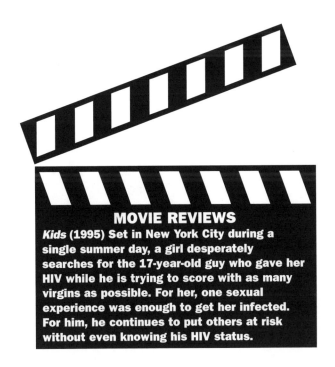

MOVIE REVIEWS

Kids (1995) Set in New York City during a single summer day, a girl desperately searches for the 17-year-old guy who gave her HIV while he is trying to score with as many virgins as possible. For her, one sexual experience was enough to get her infected. For him, he continues to put others at risk without even knowing his HIV status.

Scabies and Pubic Lice

Type: Critters

Symptoms: Extreme itching and redness in the genital area. You can sometimes see pubic lice, but scabies are too small to see without a microscope.

Treatment: Washing the body and all clothes, bedding, etc., in a special insecticide soap that you can get at the pharmacy.

If Left Untreated: The critters will go to other parts of your body and the itching will get worse!

THE GREAT POX[5]

Before penicillin was discovered, many famous people suffered from what we now believe to have been syphilis (then called the Great Pox) or its complications including:
Christopher Columbus
Al Capone (gangster)
King Henry VIII
Franz Schubert (composer)
August Strindberg (playwright)
Friedrich Nietzsche (philosopher)
Paul Gauguin (artist)

Syphilis

Type: Bacteria

Symptoms: The symptom of the primary stage of syphilis is a single firm, round, small, and painless sore (called a chancre) on the genitals. The chancre will go away on its own in one to five weeks. However, even if the sore is gone, the syphilis is not. The second stage of syphilis starts when one or more areas of the

Syphilis was the first STD where educational outreach was used to let the public know about it and its cure. These posters are from the 1960s (right) and 1940s (left).

skin break into a rash that usually does not itch. Sometimes the rashes are so faint they are not noticed. Rashes typically last two to six weeks and clear up on their own. If the syphilis still is not treated, it will go into remission, overtake the body, and eventually lead to madness, blindness, and liver failure. This last stage of syphilis is fatal.

Treatment: One dose of penicillin (an antibiotic) will cure a person who has had syphilis for less than a year. However, a person who has syphilis must not have sex with anyone until the sore is completely healed, or they will transmit the disease to their partner.

If Left Untreated: Syphilis can lead to madness, blindness, and liver failure, and eventually death.

Trichomoniasis

Type: Parasite (it works like a bacteria)

Symptoms: In women, trichomoniasis causes a frothy, yellow-green vaginal discharge with a strong odor. The genital area will also itch and appear infected. The infection may also cause discomfort during intercourse and urination. Men with symptoms may have an irritation inside the penis, mild discharge, or slight burning after urination or ejaculation.

Treatment: Trichomoniasis can usually be cured with one dose of the prescription drug metronidazole.

If Left Untreated: The itching and burning may continue until trichomoniasis is treated.

UNETHICAL SCIENCE

For forty years (1932–1972), the U.S. Public Health Service conducted experiments on almost four hundred black men in Tuskgeekee, Alabama, who had syphilis. Although penicillin had been discovered, these men were not cured of their disease because doctors wanted to examine how late-stage syphilis affected blacks as opposed to whites—the theory was that while whites died from neurological damage (i.e., they went mad), blacks, who are more prone to heart disease, would die of heart failure. Because historical documents tell us how whites from syphilis died, experiments on whites were apparently not necessary. A news journalist, Jean Heller, leaked the story in 1972, thus stopping the experiments. However, as a result of this experiment, twenty-eight men died of syphilis, one hundred died of related complications, forty wives had been infected, and nineteen children were born with the disease. It wasn't until 1997 that the government apologized for the Tuskeegee experiments, when then-president Bill Clinton said "The United States government did something that was wrong—deeply, profoundly, morally wrong."[6]

IF I DON'T SEE IT,
I DON'T HAVE IT, RIGHT?

Wrong!! It would be easy for someone to believe that if they do not see or feel any of the symptoms of an STD, then they are STD-free. Unfortunately, this is not the case. If you read closely, you saw that some STDs rarely have any symptoms (chlamydia and gonorrhea are especially sneaky). That means, you could feel perfectly fine, yet you are actually infected with an STD. Given that tidbit of information, if you had to get an STD, would you rather:

1. **Have no symptoms and feel great,**
2. **Have symptoms and burn, itch, and feel miserable.**

If you said "Have no symptoms," I would not want to be you or your sex partner. The actual answer is "Have symptoms." Sure, having symptoms is no fun, but symptoms can be a good thing. Having symptoms means you know you have the disease. Knowing you have the disease means that you know you need treatment. Knowing you need treatment means that you will hopefully get treatment. Getting treatment is not only good for you, but good for your partner, and the rest of society. Knowing you have an STD can help stop the spread of that STD. Make sense? When you get an STD, you want to have symptoms. Here's a story to help make this clearer:

> *Jeffrey has sex with a person infected with gonorrhea. After a few days, he feels awful. It burns when he pees—so bad that it feels like razor blades (I have had some people describe it to me like this). What does Jeffrey do? Does he just continue through life as if nothing were wrong? Heck no! He is going to get that checked out! And when he does, he learns that he has gonorrhea. He gets some antibiotic pills and he is cured. He tells his partner to go in for testing, who then gets treated if necessary. This chain of gonorrhea is broken, thanks to symptoms!*

Meanwhile, Monica has sex with a person infected with chlamydia. Like up to 80 percent of women, once she gets the disease, she has no symptoms. Monica feels healthy, despite the fact she has this disease, and lives her life as if nothing is wrong. A few weeks later, she falls in love with a wonderful guy at a party—they just seem to hit it off right away and they feel right together. They have sex, and she transmits the disease to him (not on purpose—she has no idea she is sick). After six great months together, they break up and start to date other people. Monica's ex, infected with chlamydia, also has no symptoms (like half of all the guys who have the disease). He has sex with other people, transmitting the disease to them (and they spread the disease to other future partners, and the chain continues). Meanwhile, Monica meets another great person and after dating for five years, they decide to marry and have children. This young couple becomes frustrated after trying to have children for a year. A doctor's exam reveals that Monica is now infertile; her fallopian tubes are scarred due to the infections caused by the chlamydia she never knew she had.

The obvious moral of the story is, symptoms may stink in the short term, but when you look at the big picture, be thankful you were one of the lucky ones who was able to get treatment for an STD. The hidden moral of the story is, *if you have sex, get tested for STDs on a regular basis* (like, once a year or even twice a year if you have unprotected sex or multiple partners). Get tested even if you feel fine. Get tested for your benefit, and the benefit of breaking one of the chains of STD transmission.

GETTING TESTED FOR STDs

So, you think you might have an STD and you want to do something about it. The next step is to get tested to see if you actually have an STD, and if so, what kind. There are basically three different types of tests that a doctor or health clinic will give you: a urine test, a blood test, or a swab test.

A urine test is when a health worker asks you to pee in a cup and then tests your urine for STDs; similarly, a blood test is when a health worker takes a sample of your blood (using a needle—it only stings for a second) and tests it. Finally, a swab test is when someone takes a sample of your cells from either your vagina or the inside of your penis using a cotton swab (Q-Tip). They put the cell sample on a slide and examine it under a microscope.

All these tests take a few days before there are results. Therefore, while you are waiting for the results of your test(s) do not have sex with anyone until you know if you are at risk for spreading a disease to someone else. Waiting is not everyone's favorite thing to do, but it's the right thing to do.

CHOOSE THE RIGHT DOCTOR FOR YOU

Doctors are great people to help you with STD testing and to discuss birth control options. As you get older, the doctor you had growing up may or may not be the best person for you. How do you tell which doctor is good for you? Consider the following things:

- Does your doctor's waiting room have interesting magazines, or is it full of stuff for only babies?
- Does your doctor let you know that everything you say is confidential, unless it is a threat to your life?
- Does your doctor allow the two of you privacy during your visit, or is a parent with you all the time?
- Does your doctor ask questions about sex, alcohol, drugs, and/or your diet? When your doctor asks questions, it is not because s/he is nosy, but because s/he cares about your health!
- Will your doctor arrange for a separate, private billing if you wish to set up a private visit between the two of you?

A teen has a right to make a confidential visit to the doctor's office—in fact, it is your right to get tested for pregnancy and/or STDs, or ask about drug use, without your parent's knowledge.

If you feel you have "outgrown" your doctor, talk to a parent about it. Your parent can call your health plan to see if there is anyone in their health plan that specializes in teens, not just kids. To find a doctor that specializes in teen—not just children's—health, go to the Society for Adolescent Medicine at www.adolescenthealth.org. In the meantime, you can drop by a health clinic to get information on STDs, birth control, or any other questions about your sexual health.

RECENT RESEARCH: CHLAMYDIA IN TEENS

The more researchers study chlamydia, the more they realize how common it is. As many as one in ten adolescent girls tested for chlamydia is infected. In fact, the cases of chlamydia in teen girls represent about half of all the chlamydia cases in the United States.[7]

SPREAD THE NEWS, NOT THE DISEASE

If you are diagnosed with an STD, you absolutely must tell your partner or partners about it. Look at it this way, if someone you were sexual with had an STD, you would want that person to tell you. Telling someone they might have a health problem and that they might be spreading it to other people is the right thing to do.

There are a few different ways you can tell someone about the STD:

1. Find a quiet time to talk. Say something like: "I care about you and I want to do what I believe is right. So, I have something to tell you. I have an STD, and that means you might have it too."
2. The clinic where you were tested for STDs might call your partner for you. Ask the clinic about their policy.
3. Write a note explaining the situation if you honestly can't face up to your partner.
4. If you are no longer in touch with your partner, write them a letter. Find that person. You are doing a good deed and helping not just you and your former partner, but many others as well. Be proud of yourself for doing a good deed.

Sex: What It Is, Who Is Doing It, What It's Like, and Other Important Questions

BASIC STATS ON WHAT IS GOING ON "OUT THERE"

There is all this talk in the news, on TV, in schools, about how teens are having sex. The coverage on the issue is to the point where it can feel as though all teens are having sex all the time. This is far from the truth. While it's true that most teens have kissed someone before (90 percent say they have), as the sexual behavior gets more intimate and serious, the number of teens who have done it decreases. When it comes to deep kissing, 79 percent say they have done it.[1] That may sound like a lot, but if you flip the percentage around that means one in five teens has not French kissed. That is a lot of people who have never done it.

Also, different people tend to do different things when it comes to sex. For example, white teens tend to have less penis–vagina sex, but more oral sex, than black teens. Asian teens tend to have sex later on in life. Hispanic teens tend to have less penis–vagina sex and engage in other sexual behaviors instead. These are generalizations to be sure—different individuals in these racial groups will have different experiences—but there are trends such as these that researchers look at.

HOW DO YOU FEEL ABOUT SEX?

You feel that everyone is having sex, you feel like you are the only one having sex, you feel as though you should be having sex. Truth is, about half of all high school students are sexually active. In fact, the level of sexual experience of teens is on the decline. So, whether you are or are not having sex, about half of your classmates are in the same boat as you are. No matter what you are doing, choosing to have or not to have sex, you are not alone.

Deciding whether or not to have sex is not a group decision; your parents, friends, favorite television show, or celebrity crush might influence your sexual decisions, but none of these should have the final say in your decision. The decision to have sex is a decision *two people*—and only two—make *together*.

What you should figure out before you have sex—whether it be the first time or the next time—is whether you and your partner *want* to have sex. The way to know if your partner wants to have sex is to ask that person (see chapter 9 on communication for tips on how to do that). And although it may sound a bit weird, the way to find out if you want to have sex is to ask yourself. Really. On a day or night when you are by yourself, take some quality time to think about how you feel about sex and other sexual behaviors. It will probably take more time than just this one session to really understand how you feel about sex, and to figure out when and under what circumstances you would and would not want to have sex with someone, but starting with just this one time is a great start. The more you think about it, the more you will know who you are and what your values are when it comes to engaging in different sexual activities. Not sure where to start? Here are some questions you can ask yourself to get you going:

- Is it okay to kiss someone on our first date?
- How far am I willing to go the first time I hook up with someone?
- What do I think is the best age to start having sex?
- Is it okay to do everything with someone except have sex?
- Do I consider having oral sex as having sex?
- What will I do if the person I am with wants to have sex and I do not want to?
- What will I do if the person I am with does not want to have sex and I want to?

You can answer these questions in your head, or you can write out your answers in a journal. Sometimes putting something in writing makes it more real, so you might want to try it. Also, know that these questions are not meant to be the only questions you should ask yourself. In fact, it's a good idea to write down the questions you have and take the time to answer them. Questions that you come up with on your own are a lot more meaningful than any questions you are going to find in a book.

And don't be worried if you do not know the answers to some of these questions right away. But if you are struggling to come up with answers, here's a suggestion: Don't put yourself in a position where you will find out the answer to this question through experience! What that means is, if you are not sure how far you are willing to go the first time you hook up with someone, it's a good idea to not hook up with someone until you have an answer. Finding out by doing often leads to regretting things you have done. Did you know that although the average age teens start having sex is just over fifteen years of age, when teens are asked what the *best* age to start having sex is, the average age is eighteen years?[2] That is a three-year difference. And three years is a lot of time for learning, growing, and understanding what a big deal sex really is.

What that statistic about sexual regret shows is that teens often have sex and then wish they had waited. Sadly, regret is a common feeling that teens have after they have sex; over half of teens who have sex wish they had waited longer before they had sex for the first time. One in four teens do not believe that the sexual experiences they have had were pleasurable. The message to take away from all of this is, it's okay to wait to have sex, if that is what you want to do. But you are not going to know how long you want to wait until you ask yourself.

RECENT RESEARCH ON THE SEXUAL BEHAVIOR OF TEENS

For the first time in thirty years, the rate of sexual activity in teens has decreased in the United States. In addition, teens who are having sex are using contraception more often, meaning that they are acting more responsibly when they are choosing to have sex. Not surprisingly, because teens are having less sex and more responsible sex, the teen pregnancy rate has also decreased for the first time in years.[3]

WHAT IS SEX?

In order to decide if you are ready to, or want to, have sex, it's a good idea to know what sex is. Don't laugh. There are a lot of people in this world, and almost all of them have a different idea as to what it means to have sex. These different ideas as to what sex is and isn't often come up when someone thinks about whether they are a virgin or not. Basically, a virgin is someone who has not had sex before. But what does that mean really? Is a person who has never had penis–vagina sex before, but has had oral sex twenty times still a virgin? Is a person who has had phone sex still a virgin? Is a person who was raped as a child a virgin?

When you think about it, the concept of virginity is not as clear as you might think.

People who choose not to have sex sometimes say that they are practicing abstinence. Again, this seems like a clear enough decision. If someone wants to be abstinent, then all they have to do is choose not to have sex. But how simple is this decision? Which sexual behaviors are an abstinent person "allowed" or "not allowed" to do? Can a person have cybersex with another and still be abstinent? Have anal sex? Give someone a hand job? Once again, a concept that seems so clear becomes a bit fuzzy when you think about it. Different people have different answers to all these questions, and no answer is more right than another.

It's important to define virginity and abstinence for yourself, and then stick to your definitions and stay true to your limits. Only you can decide what is right for you, comfortable for you, and best for you. These are the definitions of sex, abstinence, and virginity that matter the most—the ones that are thought out carefully by you.

But, no matter what your definition of virginity and abstinence are, defining these words is not only helpful for you, but also to anyone you have sex with. Why, you may ask, should you share your ideas of virginity and abstinence with a sexual partner? The answer is simple: so that you and your partner can protect and honor both of your sexual beliefs and health. For example, say that you believe that someone who has had oral sex before is no longer a virgin, but your partner believes that someone who has had oral sex and not penis–vagina sex is still a virgin. Not a big deal you say? Think again. A person who has had oral sex before is at risk for having an STD; translation, your partner, who says s/he is a virgin, potentially has an STD. The proper STD prevention may not take place and the disease could be spread. A little communication about beliefs and practices can go a long way in taking care of your health.

RECENT RESEARCH

A group of college students were asked whether the following behaviors counted as sex. Here is what they said:[4]

Behavior	% of college students who said this *was* sex
Penile–vaginal sex without orgasm	90%
Oral sex on a man with orgasm	54%
Oral sex on a man without orgasm	34%
Anal sex with orgasm	96%
Anal sex without orgasm	89%

Notice how the percentages change depending on whether or not the people involved have an orgasm and remember—just because you didn't cum doesn't mean an STD wasn't spread!

NOT ALWAYS A VALUE

Some cultures believed that a girl should lose her virginity as part of a "coming of age" ceremony. The ancient Greeks didn't think it was such a good idea to marry a virgin because they wanted to know if a woman was capable of having sex before they married her. It wasn't until the rise of Christianity when a woman's virginity carried a great deal of importance (note: the Virgin Mary). Today, there are mixed opinions as to whether a woman should remain a virgin until marriage.[5]

ARE YOU READY?

Many of you want to know an answer to a very difficult question: *How do I know when I am ready to have sex?*

Well, that question, like all difficult questions, has no one answer. However, here is a list of things that I think you must be able to do before you have sex:[6]

- ◎ **You should feel no doubt about what you are doing.**
- ◎ **You should not feel ashamed about what you are doing.**
- ◎ **You should feel comfortable talking about sexuality with your partner.**
- ◎ **You should go to a doctor or clinic and talk to someone about contraception.**
- ◎ **You should be ready and willing to have sex without having drugs or alcohol.**
- ◎ **Both you and your partner need to be willing to use condoms or another form of protection every time you have sex.**
- ◎ **You are being totally honest with your partner about your feelings, and you believe that your partner is being totally honest with you.**
- ◎ **You need to like your partner's friends and like the way your partner is around them.**
- ◎ **After you have sex, you will not feel the need to either hide the fact of what you did, nor should you feel the need to tell everyone what you did. Having sex is a private matter between you and your partner.**
- ◎ **You both need to be tested for STDs, including AIDS.**
- ◎ **You and your partner have discussed what you would do if there is a pregnancy.**
- ◎ **You really want to have sex, because you want to, not just because your partner wants to.**

Long list, huh? You bet it is. Deciding to have sex is a very big deal and deserves to have a long checklist associated with it. You are going to remember your first time for your whole life. You will hold on to that memory forever. You want it to be a pleasant, exciting, and loving memory. You deserve nothing short of that.

Another way to decide whether you are ready or not to have sex is to take yourself through the following mind exercise:

The Naked Dance

Could you do the Hokey-Pokey, naked, in front of your partner (not while high or drunk)? If you can do this and have a good time doing it, you may be ready to have sex. Why? Well, doing the Hokey-Pokey naked in front of your partner means a lot of things. It means:

- You are willing to be vulnerable in front of your partner.
- You are able to laugh at yourself.
- You are comfortable with your body.
- You trust that your partner will laugh with you and not at you.
- You trust that your partner will not tell the whole school about what you did.

And all those things count for a lot! They show comfort and trust within yourself and between you and your partner. Those are good qualities to have.

REASONS TO WAIT

- You want to get to know your partner better.
- You want to concentrate on school.
- You want to follow your religious beliefs.
- You want to learn more about safer sex.
- You don't feel ready.
- Your gut tells you to wait.

THE FIRST TIME

You have thought about it on your own. You have talked about it with your partner. The two of you, both together and individually, are ready. You want to have sex together. Having sex for the first time comes with a very strange contradiction. Although very few people find it as special or loving or dramatic as they imagine it will be, having sex for the first time is an event you will remember for the rest of your life. You will remember where you were, how it felt, when it happened, and of course who it was with. So take your first time seriously. There is only one first.

You have heard many things about "the first time" and most likely all of them are true. This is because different people have different experiences when it comes to first times. Here are some things that are true for everyone when it comes to having sex for the first time:

- A girl can get pregnant the first time she has sex with a guy: It doesn't matter whether the sex lasts three seconds or a whole hour. If there is penetration, there is a chance of pregnancy, even if neither person orgasms.

- A person can get an STD the first time they have sex: Once again, the length of time or whether there are orgasms does not matter. If one person in the couple is infected, there is a chance that that person can infect the other.

- The first time you have sex will affect your views about sex for the rest of your life. Take the time to make it a special one and choose a good partner to share it with. Sure, there may be some mistakes and awkward moments, but with an understanding partner, those "imperfections" will make your experience unique, but not necessarily embarrassing.

MOVIE REVIEW

American Pie (1999)
Four senior guys make a pact that they will lose their virginity by prom night. All the embarrassing laughs you can handle in one movie.

Here are some things that differ from couple to couple regarding having sex for the first time:

- ◎ **How long it lasts:** Many first times last only a few seconds. Others last a long time because there is a lot of foreplay and it may take a while for a body to be ready for sex. A guy's penis needs to be hard enough for the condom to fit properly, and a gal needs to be wet enough so that penetration feels good. Mutual masturbation and lubricant can help.

- ◎ **How it feels:** Some barely feel a thing—rarely does a woman have an orgasm the first time she has sex with a man. Others feel great pleasure, others intense pain. The basic rule of thumb is, if it hurts a lot, try again later. Later can either mean in a couple of minutes after more kissing takes place, or another day. Oftentimes, a female's first time having sex is very painful, either because she is not wet enough for penetration, her muscles are too tense, or her hymen is in the way. Any of these sources of pain and discomfort can be solved by making sure the gal feels relaxed, is aroused enough, and feels comfortable with what she is doing. Nervousness is a very normal part of having sex, but feeling unsafe or uncomfortable is not. If it feels wrong, it *is* wrong.

- ◎ **How the person feels afterward:** Some people feel great, others feel dreamy, and unfortunately, many don't feel so good after sex. Over half of teens in one survey (54 percent) said they should have waited until they were older before having sex for the first time. Only 5 percent said they had waited too long.

- ◎ **Whether one or both of you cum:** Very often, the guy who is penetrating will cum during a sexual encounter (however, it does not happen all of the time). This is because it's his penis that is getting the most stimulation. Special attention needs to be paid to the person who is being penetrated in order for that person to have an orgasm. And all that talk about simultaneous orgasms? Overrated—at least that is what every survey on American sex tells us.

- ◎ **Whether it will help or hurt the relationship:** Sex is a funny thing. No matter what, sex will change a relationship. For better or for worse depends on the couple and the individuals within the couple. If the sex is planned, discussed, and honest feelings are shared before and after the experience, chances are the relationship will grow closer. But if things are left

unsaid and not everyone's feelings are acknowledged, the
relationship will most likely take a turn for the worse.

?

Question:[7]

I had sex for the first time a couple of days ago. I bled
fairly badly, and it continued to bleed, off and on for a day
or two more. Is this normal?

—Seventeen-year-old female in Massachusetts

Answer:

Light bleeding for a couple of days after first sex can be
because the hymen, a piece of tissue in the vagina, has been
ruptured, or there was some minor tearing. This is normal
and should not be worried about. It can also be that there is
not enough lubrication, causing small tears in the vaginal
area. You can use a little water-based lubricant for extra
lubrication, or use prelubricated condoms. As always, if you
are concerned, or if it happens again, see your doctor.

I know you did not ask, but if you haven't already, please
see a doctor (or clinic) to get a reliable method of birth
control and use a condom every time you have vaginal or oral
intercourse to protect against sexually transmitted infections.
Good Luck!

Dr. X, *We're Talking* teen health website

HELPFUL HINTS FOR THE FIRST TIME

Here are some things to consider before having sex for
the first time—you are planning ahead, aren't you?

- Make sure you pick a private, comfortable location:
  Nothing kills the mood more than being afraid that
  you will be interrupted.

- Bring plenty of lube: A drop or two of lube in the
  condom, and plenty of lube in the partner makes
  for a more comfortable, less painful sexual
  experience.

- Have a pillow handy: For male–female sex, putting
  a pillow under the female's butt may make it feel
  more comfortable for her.

- Women on top: For male–female sex, if the female
  is on top, she can control how much of his penis
  goes in so it does not hurt so much.

CONCERNS ABOUT THE "FIRST TIME"

Having sex for the first time IS a big deal, and many people have a lot of questions about it. Most of these questions, in my experience, come from girls. Here are some questions that we asked on my advice board:

▶ Can my doctor tell if I have had sex? Will he tell my parents?

▶ I had sex for the first time and did not orgasm; is there something wrong with me?

▶ My boyfriend and I had sex for the first time, and when I woke up the next day there was blood on my underwear! Should I worry about this or get it checked?

▶ During sex, do you also kiss the person you are with?

▶ How bad will it hurt the first time I have sex? Will we have to stop because of the pain?

Oftentimes, there is no one answer to questions like this. But asking questions is a great way to start finding answers so that you are comfortable about having sex for the first time.

FAKING IT

Faking orgasms is a silly thing to do. Here's why:

1. You are perpetuating the myth that in order for sex to be good, someone has to cum. In reality, sex can be fun and fulfilling without orgasm.

2. If you keep faking it, your partner will not realize that you are not having an orgasm. Then, when you want to have an orgasm, your partner will not understand why the tried and true techniques that supposedly worked before are not effective this time around.

3. You are making it harder to communicate about sex.

4. You are being dishonest to both yourself AND your partner.

FIRST TIMES REMEMBERED

On my friend's site, Woman Links, www.womanlinks.com, adult women recall the first time they had sex:[8]

> "I was 17. It was truly anticlimactic . . . literally. I'm not sure what I expected, but it was uncomfortable. We both had been drinking and smoking pot, which I'm sure didn't help matters, but it was like the blind leading the blind! He was a college freshman and I was a senior in HS. I didn't actually begin to enjoy myself until years and a few men later."

> "I was 15. Way too young. I wish I would have waited until I was older and more able to handle everything that went along with it. The guy turned out to be a major JERK who cheated on me with everyone he met."

> "Much, much too young. If I knew then what I know now. . . . What I thought it would be like was not even remotely close to the reality. It hurt, I developed a bladder infection, and never enjoyed myself until years later.

> The idea of waiting for the right person may sound prudish, but it really would have been best."

Of course, not all first time experiences are bad. But it's important to know that first times are not always a magical event, but they are a time that you will always remember. Choose wisely!

> "I'm quite shy, and I sense the feeling that my girlfriend is ready for something more than me just making out with her. Every time we get anywhere near the topic of sex, I shy away quite a bit . . . and it used to be cute, but now I think I'm irritating her, and myself. Does anyone have any ideas that might help a guy out? I've never been in a relationship as serious as the one I'm in now—and I certainly haven't gotten this far with anyone before. I feel like I'm holding her back . . . should I speed up, tell her to slow down, or what? Any help would be much appreciated.
> Thanks,
> Hopeless

> Hopeless,
> Don't feel that you should rush it for her, or necessarily tell her to slow down. Talk to her. I know that is what most say but it's true. If you can't say it to her face, write it in a letter or email. . . . Telling her how much you feel for her and want to always be with her but the thought of sex is scaring you. Tell her you feel like that is what she is looking for and you are afraid that you're disappointing her. That will start the two of you talking about it.
> Good luck!
> BabyG

Safer Sex

WHAT IS SAFER SEX?

If you want to do everything you possibly can to not face an unwanted pregnancy or STD, there are three choices you can make:

1. Choose to not have sex,
2. Use a condom,
3. Have you and your partner get tested for STDs, and then both remain monogamous—that means, stay with each other and only each other.

In this chapter, we will spend some time looking at the first and third options. Condoms are talked about enough in chapter 7 on birth control.

CHOOSING TO NOT HAVE SEX

Choosing to not have sex is the most effective way of protecting yourself from an STD or unwanted pregnancy. But, choosing to not have sex is not as simple as it sounds. There are two parts of the decision to refrain from having sex:

1. Knowing and understanding what sexual activities you are not doing (not having sex),
2. How long you will not do those activities.

We are going to spend a lot of time talking about these two parts of your decision to postpone sexual involvement so that it's easier to understand either why this choice is right for some people but not others, and also to help those who choose not to have sex stick to their decisions despite all the pressures there are out there for people to have sex.

WHAT IS SEX? THE EXPERTS ANSWER THE QUESTION THIS TIME

ABSTINENCE

Choosing not to engage in a sexual behavior that will put you at risk for STDs or an unwanted pregnancy.

One girl wrote this question on my advice board:
- "I have had a boyfriend for two years. We have not had sex yet, but we have had oral sex a couple of times. Does that mean I am still a virgin?"

According to the CDC, the answer is NO, because she put herself at risk for STDs.

If you are going to choose to not have sex, the first thing you need to do is figure out what sex is. Sounds like a silly thing to do, but it really isn't. You see, there are many different people out there who have different ideas as to what sex is and isn't. Take people who consider themselves virgins even if they have had anal or oral sex before. Or how about someone who was raped. That person may consider herself a virgin because what she experienced was not an act of sex, but an act of violence.

So, if *you* are choosing not to have sex, that is, choosing to be abstinent, what are you deciding not to do? It sounds like a funny question, but a lot of people are confused and have different opinions about what they "can" and "cannot" do when they are choosing not to have sex.

In this book, I define what sex is by one of the reasons people choose not to have sex—for safety reasons. I use the definition of sex that the Centers for Disease Control and Prevention (CDC) use when they talk about how not to get AIDS and other STDs.[1] In a nutshell, sex is connecting any of the two body parts together shown in diagram 6.1.

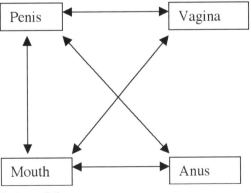

Diagram 6.1

As you can see, there are many ways that STDs can be transmitted—via the mouth, genitals, or anus. According to the CDC, these types of sexual contact all "count" as sex because they can transmit sexually transmitted diseases—especially HIV, the most dangerous and deadly STD that exists today.

If you are choosing to be abstinent—that is, if you are choosing to not have sex—I highly suggest that you use the CDC definition of sex too. That way, you and anyone you are with will stay safe and healthy.

How Long Will You Wait?

You have just read a lot about how to define sex, and therefore, abstinence—knowing what you can and cannot do when choosing not to have sex. We have defined sex in terms of what is safe for your body in terms of unwanted pregnancy and STDs. I hope you see that the word "abstinent" is not as straightforward as you may have thought it was before you picked up this book, and that you have also learned how important it is to communicate with your partner about sexual activities to make sure you are comfortable with them.

DIFFERENCES OF OPINION

In a study conducted in 1997, researchers asked college students "What is abstinence?" The researchers then listed a bunch of different sexual activities and the students either wrote a "yes" or "no" letting the researcher know whether someone could perform the sexual activity and still be practicing abstinence. Here are the percentages of people who said that you could *not* engage in this behavior if you are going to practice abstinence:[2]

French Kissing	25 percent (this behavior is abstinence according to the CDC)
Oral Sex	37 percent (this behavior is not abstinence according to the CDC)
Mutual Masturbation	39 percent (this behavior is abstinence according to the CDC)
Anal Sex	75 percent (this behavior is not abstinence according to the CDC, and one out of four people believes it is!)

So you see, different people have different definitions of what it means to be abstinent. That is one very good reason why it's important to talk about what abstinence means to you and your partner if you are choosing abstinence in your sexual relationship.

The moral of the story is, do not take someone's word for it if they say they are a "safe" person to be with because they are still a virgin. Instead, when talking to someone about safer sex, it's sometimes better to ask them if they have ever done anything that put them at risk for STDs—you can even name the behavior for them if they are not sure. That way, you can be sure about both your and your partner's sexual safety. Remember, if someone who is choosing not to have sex is still engaging in oral or anal sex, that person is *not* abstinent as far as health and safety are concerned.

Now that you are on the road to deciding what you will and will not do if you choose not to have sex—that is, be abstinent—let's look at the second part of our definition of abstinence—how long you will not do those activities.

There are many extents to which people will choose not to have sex. Some people are choosing not to have sex for a short amount of time—for example "I will choose not to have sex until I can get a hold of a condom." Others are waiting a little bit longer—until they are in love, married, or perhaps never. The point is that it's important to wait to have sex until you are in a *safe and comfortable situation*. Everyone has a different length of time that they will choose to be abstinent. It's important to decide what length of time is right for you and your partner.

Some Doors Close, Others Open

Choosing to not have sex does not mean that you cannot be sexual. There is a big difference between having sex and engaging in sexual behaviors. The message I want to convey here is: Abstinence Is Not Anti-Sex!!!!!

This may surprise you, but it won't by the time you are done reading this section. We're going to talk about some things that people CAN do with each other that can still "count" as abstinence according to some people. Remember, different people have different definitions of abstinence and all should be respected.

There are two kinds of sexual behaviors—with touching and without touching. Even without engaging in activities that involve the definition of sex according to the CDC, there are many things you can do that can be very sexual and intimate. Table 6.1 shows just a few.[3] Pretty cool list, huh? Feel free to add to it, or take away from it, depending on your definition of abstinence. The point is, you can express your feelings for someone without having sex. Anyone who says that abstinence is "no fun" just might be lacking in creativity, the ability to express themselves, and imagination.

Being sexual with touching	Being sexual without touching

Kissing someone on the
    Lips
    Ear
    Belly Button
    Shoulder
	Say something
	    Mushy
	    Loving
	    Sexy
	    Flirty

Touch someone so that they barely feel it	Make eye contact and smile
Hug them real tight	Blow in their ear
Play with their hand as you hold it	Write a letter that says how you feel
Trace your name in their back	Send a surprise gift to share later
Exchange massages	Flirt!
Put your hand on their leg or knee when you're talking	

INTIMACY: DON'T KNOCK IT 'TIL YOU'VE TRIED IT

You've heard it before, but I will say it again—teens in today's society are given mixed messages about sex. On the one hand, they are told to "just say no" to sex, while on the other hand they are bombarded—lambasted even—with glorifying sexual images from the media and are often given the message that sex makes them more mature. Sex, in many ways, is considered the "be all end all" in relationships, and may even be considered the reason to be in a relationship in the first place—at least that is what so many of those beer commercials would have you believe.

But guess what? There is a *lot* more to a relationship than just having sex. In fact, it's more than possible to have a *great* relationship with someone, and not even have sex with that person. It's also possible to have a pretty crummy relationship with someone, even if you are having sex. In this section,[4] we are going to look at the differences between *sex* and *intimacy*. In fact, I am going to make the point that if the goal of a relationship is to be intimate with another person, then that relationship will be a lot healthier for everyone involved.

An intimate relationship is a close, mature relationship that may or may not include sex. Most people do not see intimacy as the goal of a relationship, or even a fun evening—they think sex should be the end result. When someone comes up to you after a party and says "so, did you get any last night?" they are not talking about cuddling, kissing, and "quality time." They are talking about sex. So if you answer: "Yeah, I really got to know this person really well and I think I actually like her! We talked about our families and then spent about half an hour tracing messages on each other's back," people are gonna look at you strange. Yet if someone who had sex, even though it lasted only two minutes, answers: "Yeah, I got some," or "We got nasty really quick!" that person is the one who gets the attention in the locker room or during lunchtime gossip.

It seems that sex, no matter how quick and unfulfilling, may be seen as a bigger deal in people's eyes than a truly intimate moment where everyone's clothes stay on. Here is another example of that: What do we call sexual behaviors (besides sex itself), such as kissing, and touching? We call it foreplay. And what does foreplay mean? Fore means "before," so foreplay is "before play." And what would the "play" be in this case? The play is "sex." So if you think of all these things you can do with someone that are very close, pleasurable, and intimate as foreplay, they sort of lose their own meaning, even though kissing, touching, and simply spending time together can be very special to someone.

Batter Up! The Baseball Approach to Sex

Currently, many people think about sexual expression and activity using some form of the Baseball Approach to Sex. In this approach, the place where a couple starts their relationship is "sexual inexperience," and the end point or goal of the relationship is to have *sex*!! By making sex the goal, it becomes the focal point of sexual expression, a couple's time together, and therefore the relationship.

Phrases like "Going all the way," and "Home run" come from the mind-set of this way of thinking. Along the way to having sex, people progress along the bases toward intercourse: getting to first base means kissing; second base means above-the-waist touching; third base, below-the-waist touching. All of these sexual behaviors are seen as "foreplay" and therefore don't count as much as sex, the final goal.

There are some problems with thinking about sex as the goal of a relationship. First of all, it makes sex more of an accomplishment rather than a shared experience. Sex becomes a social, not a personal, reason to be in a relationship if you believe in the Baseball Approach. Second, you can barely even know a person in order to reach the goal of sex. How wonderful—or safe—is it to have sex with someone whose last name you do not know?

Another thing, if people consider sex the goal of a relationship, they can go at it without really talking to each other about what they do and do not like. Partners are not encouraged to talk about their desires or comfort levels, and may not find a good time to say when they are no longer feeling okay about what they are doing. This lack of communication can cause problems ranging from an unpleasurable experience to more serious issues such as date rape.

Getting to Know You: The Intimate Approach to Sex

Instead of seeing sex from the Baseball Approach, sexual expression can be thought about using an approach that focuses on intimacy. Here, the object of the relationship is not necessarily a sexual goal—instead, the goal of this continuum is to be intimate with another person. By making intimacy, and not sex, the goal of a relationship, you are not limiting the ways you can be with someone, but instead are opening the door to different forms of sexual expression *and* emotional expression. A relationship can become a lot more interesting, fun, and meaningful this way.

Placing intimacy as the goal of sexual expression emphasizes closeness for all involved and encourages communication between partners regardless of gender or level of sexual experience. So in this way, if sex is a part of the relationship, both partners are more likely to enjoy the sexual experience since, as a part of intimacy, you are talking about your experiences and likes and dislikes together.

This way of thinking about sexual expression encourages communication between sexual partners, because communication about your thoughts, feelings, and who you are is a big part of being intimate with another person. Even though you might choose not to have sex in a relationship, there are many ways to be intimate with your partner that do not involve sexual behavior of any kind.

So why do I think the Intimacy Approach is better than the Baseball Approach to a relationship? First off, the Intimacy Approach is the most flexible—there are so many ways to be intimate with another person. Some include sexual intercourse and some do not. You can even choose to not have sex and have a great, intimate relationship with another. In fact, having sex isn't "all that" when thinking about intimacy, because you can certainly have sex with

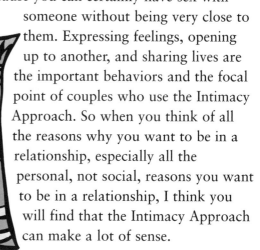

someone without being very close to them. Expressing feelings, opening up to another, and sharing lives are the important behaviors and the focal point of couples who use the Intimacy Approach. So when you think of all the reasons why you want to be in a relationship, especially all the personal, not social, reasons you want to be in a relationship, I think you will find that the Intimacy Approach can make a lot of sense.

CASUAL SEX

There is not that much information about casual sex and teens, but it's worth mentioning. Either through personal experiences or the rumor mill, you hear of people randomly hooking up at a party and going "all the way." Well, what are those experiences like? Are they fun? Safe? A good idea? What makes the casual hookup so seemingly popular?

Some numbers may help us paint a picture of casual sex among young people. In one college, less than 40 percent of the students said they had casual sex. And of those, almost 70 percent—way more than half—said that either drugs or alcohol were involved when they "did the deed." Just over half used contraception of any kind (yikes!). And of those that did have casual sex, less than half said they would do it again if they had the chance. However, more than half said they did not regret the experience.[5]

So what does this all mean? It looks like casual sex is not as common as one may think. In fact, only about one in three college students say they have ever had a one-night stand. It also appears that casual sex is not all that great if less than half would repeat the experience if given the chance. And the high amounts of drugs and alcohol used combined with the low rate of contraception use adds up to the fact that casual sex is not all that safe an experience. So, is it worth the risk? Only you can decide, but the numbers suggest the answer is "no."

BEING SAFE THROUGH TESTING AND MONOGAMY

Being monogamous means staying with one and only one partner.

There are two parts to this safer sex strategy. The first part is to make sure you and your partner do not have any STDs in the first place, and then once the coast is clear, the two of you need to be monogamous and stay monogamous so that you do not put yourself at risk for getting an STD from someone else.

The Easy Part: Getting Tested for STDs

The ONLY WAY to know if you have an STD or not is to get tested for STDs. The only way you are going to know if your partner has an STD or not is to have your partner get tested, and then trust that that person is going to tell you the truth about their results.

Where to Go?

There are two places where you can go to get tested for STDs—a doctor's office and a clinic. There is a difference between a doctor's office and a clinic when it comes to being tested for STDs. Getting tested at a doctor's office is confidential, while getting tested at a clinic is anonymous. What is the difference between an anonymous and confidential test? A confidential test is like a secret—someone promises they will not tell, but there is a way to find out the facts. A confidential test means that although no one is supposed to tell the results of your test, your name is attached to test results and it goes on a record. On the other hand, an anonymous test means you have a fake name and there is no way anyone can link you to the test results but yourself. So, if it's important for you to have your test results be anonymous, and not just confidential, you are probably better off going to a health clinic to get tested. But not all clinics give anonymous tests, so ask before you assume anything.

CLINIC VERSUS DOCTOR'S OFFICE

Other possible differences between going to a clinic and your doctor's office:

▶ **Insurance possibilities and problems:** you may be covered under your insurance, but parents may see a bill.

▶ **Cost:** Clinics can be cheaper if you do not have insurance.

▶ **Doctor trust:** If you know and trust your doctor, that person may be someone you want to talk about STDs with. But, if your parents know your doctor well, you may not want to get tested at your parent's friend's office, know what I mean?

▶ **Scheduling differences are possible:** Some places are easier to get an appointment than others.

▶ **Counseling:** Health clinics often have counseling available, especially for HIV testing—an extra bonus!

What Will Happen When I Get There?

There are two different ways to get tested for STDs—a blood test (usually done for HIV tests, but also some other STDs require blood tests) and cell sample tests.

Giving Blood for a Good Cause

When you go to a clinic to get an HIV test, or other STD blood test, a trained medical professional will take a sample of blood from your arm, tell you when the results of your test will be ready (usually a week or two), and then you go home. Be sure to ask them if you need to come back to the clinic to get your test results or if you are able to get them by calling. If you can, it's always a good idea to get your test results in person, because that way you can ask questions and get help right away if you need to. *If you find out you have an STD— Congratulations! Now you can either get it cured before more serious complications occur, or you can do your very best not to infect someone else, or even reinfect yourself!*

If the test is anonymous (remember, that means *no one* knows who you really are), you will either give a fake name or get an ID code when you call to make an appointment. This name or code will be the only name by which people know you. You may be asked to fill out some forms or surveys, but at no point should anyone ask you to put your actual name on it. Then, after the test is done, you may get a slightly different ID code in order to get the results, or you will use the same code or name as the first time. The people at the clinic will let you know.

No Blood Necessary

Another way people are tested for STDs is by giving a sample of their cells from their genital area. For girls, this means that their gynecologist or a nurse practitioner will take a cotton swab and brush the inside of the vagina. Then, the cells are put on a slide or in a tube and analyzed in a laboratory. Like blood tests, it takes a while to get the results, so be sure to ask when the results will be available.

For boys, the inside of the urethra (the hole you pee out of) is brushed to get some sample cells.

The Harder Part: Staying Monogamous and Trusting Your Partner Will Do the Same

You got the easier part out of the way—you and your partner were tested for STDs and you now both know with confidence that you are both STD free! So, now you two can have sex and not worry about catching anything— right? WRONG! The two of you now have to trust each other and yourselves enough to know that you will not be sexual with anyone else except each other. Remember—you do not necessarily have to have sex to get an STD (herpes, for example, can be passed mouth to mouth)—so being with only one partner for any sort of sexual contact is a must for this to work.

Talk to your partner. Know your partner (for more than a week or so). Listen to yourself and trust your instincts. If your partner is not even willing to get tested for STDs in the first place, that is a good sign that this is not a good safer sex method for the two of you. If you know your partner has cheated in the past (maybe that is even how the two of you started going out in the first place), then maybe this method is not the right one for you—at least not for a very long time. Remember, you could literally be putting your life into someone's hands by having unprotected sex. Be very choosy about who that person is.

REALITY CHECK
Remember, you still have to use contraception when you have sex if you do not want a pregnancy to happen! That's what birth control pills, cervical caps, and all those other methods in chapter 7 are for!

WHAT CHOICE ARE YOU GOING TO MAKE?

You now know quite a bit about the three healthy and safer sex choices that are available to you. To recap, they are:

1. **Choosing to not have sex,**
2. **Using a condom,**
3. **Having both you and your partner get tested and stay monogamous.**

Which choice is best for you? Close your eyes, think about it and decide. Then, say it out loud. And write it down. The more actively involved you are in making this decision, the more likely you are to stick with it. Next, choose a backup. What is your second choice on the list? If you opted for choice 2 for your first strategy, but no condoms are available, *then* what are you going to do? Having both a plan "A" and a plan "B" helps ensure that you will have a happier, healthier life.

By choosing a plan and a backup plan, you are miles ahead of not only most teens, but most adults too.

THE SAFEST SEX OF ALL: MASTURBATION

LOVE AND TRUST[6]

Love and trust may often go hand in hand, but they are NOT the same thing. You can love someone you do not trust (like your baby brother playing with your prized CD collection) and you can trust someone you do not love (like a judge or a teacher). So, just because you love someone, or are in love with someone, does not mean that you necessarily trust someone to stay monogamous or to be STD-free if they have not been tested. Don't let someone manipulate you by saying, "Why do we need to use a condom? Don't you *love* me?" If it's true, you can smile back and say that indeed you love that person, but you love you and your life even more and want to play it safe for now.

Of course there are times for everyone when a sexual partner is not available. During those times, some people choose to masturbate as a means of sexual release. Next to abortion, it seems as though masturbation is the sexual issue that creates the biggest stir. People will talk about sex, the importance of postponing sexual involvement, and how we need to improve sex education in schools. On television, shows will talk about affairs, "quickies," and many other sexual encounters.

But who talks about masturbation? No one, it seems. But there are a lot of myths and rumors about it. And if someone dares to break the silence around this topic, they more often than not pay dearly for it. (The all-female band the Divinyls shocked the world with their hit single "I Touch Myself" [1991].) Like the one that says girls who masturbate are nymphomaniacs (girls who are addicted to sex). Boys, if you will, "get off" more easily; they have a bit more freedom to talk about masturbation, and it's more acceptable for them to admit doing it. But even then, there are limitations. Boys who masturbate aren't getting any action in the real world, so they have to resort to pleasuring themselves. Boys who don't masturbate actually have a sex life—those who do masturbate do so because they don't have any "offers." Of course, these assumptions aren't true. Both boys and girls masturbate (and both boys and girls do not masturbate). They masturbate whether or not they have a partner, and their masturbation does not mean they are addicted to sex.

Masturbation—What It Is and Is Not

So, despite its bad rap, there are many good things about masturbation. Here are some of them:

- ◎ **It's 100 percent safe for people to do. By masturbating, you will not get pregnant, nor will you get an STD (and you will not go blind, sterile, or insane either).**
- ◎ **People who masturbate know their bodies better. They can tell if there is something wrong "down there" because they are looking! And if you notice something wrong, you can go to a doctor to take care of it.**
- ◎ **Knowing your body well also has another advantage—you know what does and does not work for you sexually. Knowing this can lead to better sexual communication between you and your current or future partner. Better communication is one of the most important factors in a healthy sex life.**
- ◎ **Masturbating can make you more comfortable with your body. And being more comfortable with your body can make you more comfortable with yourself.**
- ◎ **Masturbation helps people who choose to abstain from sexual intercourse for any reason. It's a good way to achieve sexual release because it can't hurt anyone, and it can help keep your impulses in check so you don't find yourself doing something you don't really want to do or aren't ready for.**

Of course, nothing in life is 100 percent good. There are some downsides to masturbation as well:

- ◎ **Some people who masturbate may feel guilty. They feel bad about it because they have been told by their parents or** their religion that masturbation is wrong. People who feel guilty about masturbation need to think about the reasons they feel guilty and come to terms with their decisions. If they decide to continue masturbating, knowing that they may not always agree with their family or church and that that does not make them a bad person may help. If they decide not to masturbate, they can feel comfortable knowing they have the continued acceptance of the support systems in their life regarding that issue.

◎ There *are* a few people who masturbate too much. These people masturbate to the point where their schooling and social life suffer. This situation is very rare, but it does happen. There is no set amount of times one should or should not masturbate that is healthy. If you are able to continue to have a social life complete with outside activities and friendships, and your schoolwork is not suffering because of the time you are spending masturbating, you are not masturbating too much.

So, you might want to try masturbating, but are not sure how to go about it. Basically, masturbation is touching, rubbing, or otherwise stimulating your genitals (penis for boys, clitoris for girls) in ways that feel good to you. Although I am not going to tell you exactly how, here are some pointers to consider:

◎ Make sure you are in a private place where no one can disturb you. Lock doors.

◎ Make yourself comfortable. It's important that you are in a physical place where you can be comfortable.

◎ Allow yourself to have whatever sexual fantasies you like. Fantasies are not bad, and do not necessarily reflect what you want to do in real life. Fantasies are what they are— thoughts in your head. Let them go.

◎ Use some lubricant to help your fingers. Your body will probably respond better to your touch if there is less friction. A water-based lubricant can help (saliva also works in a pinch).

◎ Do whatever feels good. There is no right or wrong way to masturbate. Experiment with different speeds, pressures,

HISTORICAL PERSPECTIVES: THE JADED HISTORY OF MASTURBATION

Today, health experts know that there are no harmful biological effects to masturbating. However, this was not the belief in the late 1700s and into the 1800s. In fact, back then, masturbation was referred to as "self-abuse" and "self-pollution" and was believed to result in long-term health problems, including insanity. Masturbation was considered especially dangerous for younger males (back then, doctors did not really believe that females masturbated at all!) because it would stunt their growth and make them unable to have children later in life. In 1886, John Harvey Kellogg (the inventor of Corn Flakes), in his book on health, mentions that masturbation is "one of the most destructive evils ever practiced."[7]

It wasn't until the 1950s that health experts realized and admitted that masturbation had no bad health effects, but still mainly considered it to be practiced by males only. Others back then did acknowledge that some females masturbated, but believed that if they did, it may "make more difficult the adjustments to the marriage partner"[8]—that is, if a girl masturbated before marriage, that she may have trouble engaging in sex with her future husband.

Today, for the most part, health experts all finally agree that the only consequences of masturbation are psychological, resulting from possible guilt or anxiety if the person who is masturbating believes it's wrong according to his or her religion or parental beliefs. However, masturbation is hardly considered an acceptable topic for discussion. Take the recent case of former surgeon general Jocelyn Elders. Elders was forced to resign in 1995 because of her controversial opinions on sex education, including her belief that masturbation is a healthy part of a young person's sexuality, and therefore it should be taught in schools.

The controversy continues . . .

and thoughts. Only you know what works for you; the only "right" things to do are the things that feel good to you.

- It's okay if you do not masturbate to orgasm. For some (usually, but not always, females) it will take a few tries before you figure out how to orgasm through masturbation. Others may simply not care to reach orgasm—they just want to get aroused, and then they stop.

Masturbation can help you realize that sex does not always mean penis-in-vagina intercourse. Learning about how your body works, discovering what your body does and does not like, and being in charge of your sexual desires are important skills to have. But, the most important thing to remember is only do what you feel comfortable doing. If masturbating is not for you, there is no reason to start.

ABOUT JOCELYN ELDERS

Elders was born in rural Arkansas in 1933, where she worked with her seven brothers and sisters in the fields. Always a top student, in 1960 she got her medical degree from the University of Arkansas (one of just three minority students to do so). She then became chief pediatric resident. In 1987, Bill Clinton (then governor of Arkansas) named her director of the state's Department of Health. When Clinton became president, he named her surgeon general. She was made to resign in 1995 (less than a year later) because of her controversial opinions about sex ed. Still a supporter of teen sex education, she is now a professor at the University of Arkansas Medical Center.

Birth Control Options

7

There are a lot of ways to try to prevent yourself from having a baby and becoming a parent. In order to make it easier for you to choose the right method for you, the birth control options in this chapter are broken down into four different categories: (1) controlling your behavior; (2) using a barrier; (3) using artificial hormones; (4) having surgery. Some ways are more effective than others. Some ways help prevent not only pregnancy, but also STDs. Reading about all the different methods can help you decide which is right for you.

As a friendly reminder, I want to reinforce that preventing pregnancy and preventing STDs are not always the same thing. While there are many ways to prevent pregnancy, and a few ways to prevent STDs that you read about in chapter 6, *there are only two things you can do to prevent both STDs and an unwanted pregnancy*. Those two ways are:

1. **Choosing not to have sex**

2. **Using a condom (though this method is not 100 percent effective, it comes pretty close)**

Because these two options take care of both fears of getting an STD and unwanted pregnancies, they are talked about more in depth than the other birth control options. Getting rid of two concerns with one action is pretty efficient, so choosing not to have sex or using a condom if you decide to have sex are pretty good choices in my book.

CONTROLLING YOUR BEHAVIOR: IT'S ALL UP TO YOU

One way to prevent yourself from getting pregnant is to stop yourself from doing things that will cause you to get pregnant. We should all know by now that the only way to cause pregnancy is for a sperm to fertilize an egg. And although modern science has created many ways for this to happen, the only way this fertilization happens that concerns us is by having penis–vagina sex that causes the guy to ejaculate while the girl is ovulating. So, how can we control our behavior so this does not happen? There are four ways to do it without using contraception—leaving it to chance, choosing not to have sex, using the withdrawal method, and using the rhythm method. Not all of these ways work all that well, as you will find out. See which ones are good options, and which ones are not worth the paper they are written on.

FACT

Forty percent of dating teens who are having sex with their partners say that they used contraception every time they have sex. That is a lot of people who are not being as safe as they could be![1]

Chance

One way to try to not get pregnant is to have sex and just hope. This is the most ineffective method of birth control around. In fact, if you just leave it to chance, there is an 85 percent chance that a pregnancy will occur. That is more than eight times out of ten. That is a lot. Simply put, prayer and luck do not work in the long run. Sure, it may work one time, maybe even two or three. But make this a habit, and you will make a baby.

In sum . . .

How it works—It doesn't.
What makes it a good choice—nothing at all.
Why it might not be right for you—you are smarter than that.
How to get it—don't need to, don't want to.
Cost—$1,000,000—the price to raise a child.
Wait time until it works—eternity.

How well does it work—not at all.
What can go wrong—everything.

Withdrawal

Withdrawal is a commonly used, but ineffective way for people to prevent pregnancy. It happens when the guy removes his penis from his partner before he cums. Problem is, there are many reasons why this method can go wrong very quickly. First, the guy has to be in total control of his ejaculation and not every guy is—he could cum sooner than he thinks and not "pull out" in time. Second, tiny drops of pre-ejaculate, or pre-cum, come out of the penis before ejaculation. This pre-cum sometimes has sperm and STD germs in it, so it is possible that a partner can still get pregnant or infected. Finally, a guy can change his mind and cum inside his partner anyway.

In sum . . .

How it works—the guy removes his penis before
  ejaculation.
What makes it a good choice—it's better than nothing—
  barely.
Why it might not be right for you—you are smarter than
  that.
How to get it—don't want to.
Cost—free, but it's a big gamble.
Wait time until it works—forever.
How well does it work—it fails 20 percent of the time.
What can go wrong—guy can cum inside by mistake,
  pre-cum carries infections and sperm.

Natural Family Planning

The concept behind the natural family planning is that a woman learns about her body and pays attention to its signals enough to know when she is going to ovulate. The theory goes that if a woman knows when she is about to ovulate, then she can know when she is and is not fertile, and thus knows when to have sex in order to have a baby or avoid having a baby.

However, like most theories, this one has its loopholes. And, like all contraceptive methods, this one has a failure rate—one that is particularly high for teens. This is because natural family planning requires a woman to have a regular menstrual cycle that is very predictable and very dependable. For the most part, teens simply do not have a regular menstrual cycle. There is too much growing, stress, and newness to the whole thing for it to be really settled. Plus, in order to really understand the natural family planning method, and to really get to know her cycle inside and out, a woman should go to a class (through a church, health clinic, or hospital) for up to *two years*. That is a long time and a lot of dedication in order to avoid a pregnancy. Thus, natural family planning is not a recommended form of birth control for teens.

In sum . . .

How it works—a woman checks out her cervical mucus, body temperature, and menstrual calendar to try to figure out when she is going to become pregnant.

What makes it a good choice—a woman gets to know her body very well, there are some religions that only accept this form of birth control.

Why it might not be right for you—it's a very unreliable method for teens because of their unpredictable menstrual cycles, it takes a long time to learn, there is NO protection against STDs.

How to get it—take a class and read a lot in order to truly understand how it works.

Cost—classes vary in price.

Wait time until it works—two years.

How well does it work—it fails up to 20 percent of the time.

What can go wrong—the woman's menstrual cycle is irregular and thus she ovulates when she does not expect to. A man's sperm can live up to six days inside the woman, thus "hanging" around until the ovulation and fertilizing the egg.

Choosing *Not* to Have Sex

Some people call choosing not to have sex "abstinence." According to the dictionary, to "abstain" from something means "to refrain deliberately and often with an effort of self-denial from an action or practice." So does that mean if someone decides to not have sex they need a lot of "effort" and are engaging in "self-denial"? That sort of talk makes abstinence sound hard or even impossible! And we know that is not true. Many people do not have sex and feel completely fine and comfortable with their decision. Indeed, they feel deep down that it's the right thing for them to do.

This is why I do not use the term "abstinence" in this book. It sounds like a bad thing. Instead, I like to think of people who are not having sex as people who are *choosing* not to have sex. They are making a personal decision. They are in control. They are proud of their behavior and what it represents.

As we have all heard a million times over from many different places (school, the news, parents, etc.), choosing not to have sex is the most effective form of birth control. We hear this over and over again because it's a true statement. If a person does not have sex, they will not get pregnant.

But as all things are, this basic statement is not as simple as you may think. In order for choosing not to have sex to be 100 percent effective, it has to be practiced correctly— that means it has to be done each and every time you are in a sexual situation. There is no such thing as practicing abstinence some of the time. But, it's easy to see that the best of intentions sometimes do not go as planned. In fact, studies show that teens who choose to not have sex do not always follow through on their plans. Up to 25 percent of teens who say they are not having sex actually change their minds (or at least their behaviors) and do have sex after all.[2]

So what does this mean? It means that choosing not to have sex is only as effective as the person using the method of birth control. Used "correctly"—that is, if the person truly does not have sex, then no pregnancy will occur. But used "incorrectly"—in other words, if a person has sex even if they say they will not—then a pregnancy can happen if a backup method is not used.

There is another tricky part to choosing not to have sex. If you choose to not have sex, you have to ask yourself "for *how long* am I choosing not to have sex?" Some people will choose not to have sex for their entire lives; people such as priests and nuns make this sort of decision. Other people choose not to have sex until they reach a certain time in their life—marriage, graduation from high school, or until they are at least twenty years old. Others wait until a certain situation comes along—they fall in love, they truly trust a person, they feel mature enough to handle the consequences. Finally, there are those who simply choose not to have sex because of logistics—there is no condom at this time, they are drunk and want to make a decision to have sex when their head is clearer, they are in a public place. As you can see from these examples, some people are choosing not to have sex for a short amount of time, while others are waiting a little bit longer. The point is that it's important to wait to have sex until you are in a safe, comfortable, and pleasant situation. Everyone has a different length of time that they will choose to be abstinent. It's important to decide what length of time is right for you and your partner.

In sum . . .

> *How it works*—a person chooses not to engage in the one behavior that will cause pregnancy.
> *What makes it a good choice*—if done properly, it's 100 percent effective against pregnancy *and* STDs.
> *Why it might not be right for you*—you may feel ready to have sex.
> *How to get it*—you get the ability to not have sex from the strength inside you.
> *Cost*—free!
> *Wait time until it works*—no wait. It works right away!
> *How well does it work*—as well as the people involved with each other.
> *What can go wrong*—something happens that makes a person have sex even when they chose not to.

BARRIERS: KEEPING THE SPERM AWAY

Barrier methods of birth control work by preventing sperm from getting near the egg. No contact between the sperm and the egg equals no pregnancy. Cool thing about these methods is that they can also help prevent the spread of STDs the same way they prevent pregnancy. A "wall" does it all.

Barrier methods are used at or near the time people are having sex. They do not remain on or inside the body the way hormonal methods do. If you are a person who does not have sex all that often, but wants to be prepared, barrier methods might be the right method for you.

Condom

Condoms have been used by millions of couples for over a century for the purpose of preventing pregnancies and the spreading of sexually transmitted diseases. Condoms are a latex covering for the penis. Latex is a type of rubber that is also used to make surgical gloves and other protective barriers. Condoms are good to use during sex because they protect against both pregnancy and STDs. You can also use them for all kinds of sex—oral, anal, and vaginal. Also, condoms are pretty cheap and you can get them without a prescription from your doctor.

In this section, we are going to take an extra close look at condoms, how they work, and how to use them effectively. We are going to give this form of birth control the most attention because it's one of the three methods of safer sex, along with choosing not to have sex and testing plus monogamy.

HISTORY OF CONDOMS

Condoms have been around for quite some time. There are cave paintings of condoms in France. The ancient Egyptians used condoms made of linen around 1000 B.C. These linen condoms were tested in the 1500s in Italy—it was found that those people who used them did not get syphilis. Thus, it was officially proved that condoms helped prevent the spread of STDs. The latex condoms of today were first available in the 1880s, although they were not commonly used until the 1930s. Today, 8.5 billion condoms are manufactured worldwide every year.

For a complete timeline, check out http://www.avert.org/condoms.htm.

Where Can You Get Condoms?

Condoms are the easiest birth control method to get a hold of (besides choosing not to have sex). You can get condoms at health or family planning clinics, drugstores, grocery stores, the doctor's office, convenience stores, special condom stores, and even in vending machines.

Lubricant—The Condom's Best Friend

It's possible—very likely even—that you have heard of condoms before picking up this book. Even if you have never seen one or used one, condoms are advertised in magazines and on the radio. They are talked about in public service announcements concerning the prevention of AIDS. However, it's rare that people talk about lubricants, which are an important part of condom use.

Sexual lubricants are *water-based* substances that reduce friction during sex. Reducing *some* friction during sex can be a good thing because it can prevent the condom from tearing and it can make sex more comfortable and pleasurable. Sexual lubricants have to be *water-based* because other types of lubricants—those that are *oil-based*— actually *eat away at latex* and make holes in condoms. What are some examples of *oil-based* lubricants? (lotion, Vaseline, cooking oil, shortening). It's important to make sure that the lubricant you use is *water-based*. You can find water-based lubricants where condoms are sold. Common brand names of lubricant include: Wett, Probe, Astroglide, and KY Jelly.

How to Be a Condom Savvy Person

Look at the condom still in its wrapper. It should have an expiration date on it. Make sure the condom you use is not expired. Expired condoms are more likely to tear, or may already have a hole in them. You do not drink expired milk, you do not use expired condoms.

Store your condoms properly. Condoms need to be kept in a *cool dry* place when not in use. They should not be kept in a car, where the heat can get really intense, or in a pocket where they can get crumpled up and also hot, being close to your body. Girls might have an easier time storing condoms because they have purses, but jacket pockets and front shirt pockets are okay places to put condoms for convenient access. Just keep them out of your pants pockets where the condom can get too close to the body.

Putting on a Condom—Do's and Don'ts for the Safest Time Possible

Now, the moment has come, and you are ready to put the condom on. How do you do it? It's easy, once you get the hang of it, but read on to learn some great pointers on the process.

Step 1: Opening the package.
First, make sure that the penis is hard before you put the condom on. Condoms do not stay on unless the penis is hard.
Push the condom to the other side of the package and carefully tear the opposite corner. No teeth, no ripping with abandon, as you do not want to tear the condom.

Step 2: Upside down versus right side up.
Before you unroll the condom, take a second to look at it. There is a right way and a wrong way to unroll the condom (yes there is). Check out figure 7.1 to see what we mean.
Unrolling the condom the wrong way will increase the chance of tearing it, so take that extra moment to make sure you are doing it right.

Putting on a Condom: The right and wrong way to do it

YES!

NO!

101

Step 3: Get out the lubricant.

Next, put a *few* drops—three or four is plenty—of lube on the *inside* of the condom (don't overdo it here, things could get too slippery and messy). You want to put lube inside the condom because it reduces the chance of the condom breaking. Also, the lubricant increases pleasure for the person wearing the condom because lubricant actually helps transmit the heat of sex through the latex of the condom.

Step 4: Putting it on.

Now you know the right direction the condom goes on the penis and you have it all lubed up. You are ready to put it on. With one hand, pinch the tip of the condom (that little nub at the top) to leave room at the top. Why do you want to do this? To leave room for the semen/cum/ejaculate. You also want to leave room at the tip of the condom so that it's more comfortable for the person wearing the condom.

Then, with other hand, form an "okay" sign, and roll the condom down *all the way* to the base of the penis, while still pinching the tip of the condom. The "okay" method decreases the chances of tearing the condom with fingernails.

Once the condom is on, the condom will have lots of room at the tip for the semen, but the rest of it's on snugly so that it will not fall off.

Finally, you can put lubricant on the outside of the condom for other partner's pleasure and to help prevent the condom from tearing.

Pretty simple, huh? *But* taking the condom off properly is just as important as putting it on properly, so thus continues the lesson. . . .

Step 5: Taking the condom off.

There are two things to remember about taking the condom off: First, do it right after the guy cums, because after ejaculation, the penis starts to get limp and the condom will no longer stay on and you don't want to spill the cum inside **the** partner.

Second, you want to grab the base of the condom and pull it off. If the guy simply pulls out without holding on to the condom, the condom can stay inside his partner and spill semen. The whole point of wearing the condom is foiled!

Finally, tie the condom like a balloon so nothing spills out of it and throw it away. Do not flush the condom down the toilet as condoms can clog toilets (and possibly leave you with either a large plumbing bill or at least some explaining to do).

One final kernel of knowledge before I declare you a condom expert: Condoms can be used once and only once. As soon as someone either loses their erection or ejaculates (or both) that condom cannot be used again! Once a condom is used, you should throw it away properly, as described above. If you want to have sex again, you must get a new condom.

You now know how to put a condom on properly and take it off successfully so that it can be an effective way to prevent pregnancy *and* STDs. Congratulations!

Which Condom Should I Use?

So, you have decided to have sex and have talked to your partner about protection. The two of you have decided to use a condom to protect yourselves against STDs and/or pregnancy. Congratulations! That is a good step toward safer sex. But then you ask—what condoms should you use? While there are many brands of condoms—Lifestyles, Trojan, Kimono, Beyond 7, Maxx— just to name a few, you should know that *all* condoms pass very strict quality control tests before they are allowed to be sold in the United States. If you buy a condom in the United States, no matter what country it was made in, you can be assured that it has been tested for strength, durability, and everything else you might be concerned about.

? Question:[3]

My boyfriend and I are getting really close. We have been talking about sex and we both agreed we would never have sex without a condom. However, neither of us knows what size condoms come in and how sizing works. . . . Could you help us?

—Sixteen-year-old female

Answer:

All condoms are not the same. Condoms come in different thicknesses, with different shapes (i.e., the same width from top to bottom, smaller at the bottom, contoured, reservoir tip, etc.), ribbed or dotted (inside or out), lubricated or nonlubricated, and in different colors.

Only you can decide what is pleasurable for you. I would encourage you to try different condoms until you find the one you like the best. Many people like the microthin condoms for enhanced sensation, and you may like condoms that have ribbing or dots on the inside, which also enhance sensation.

An important thing about using condoms is to remember to use adequate lubrication to decrease friction and enhance pleasure. You can use a drop or two of water-based lubricant (like KY Jelly, Millennium, Probe, etc.) on the inside of the condom to enhance your pleasure, and a drop or two outside the condom to increase your partner's pleasure and reduce friction.

Good for you for thinking about this!

Dr. X, *We're Talking* teen health website

Avoid Breakage!

So, if condoms have to undergo all these quality control tests, why do so many people hear and have their own stories about condoms breaking? For the most part, the reasons condoms break are *not* because they are faulty, or made wrong, but because of *human* error. The people using the condoms do things that make breakage more likely. The most common reasons condoms break are:

1. The person wearing the condom did not leave enough room at the tip. When a condom is rolled onto the penis, the person should leave some room at the top of the condom. This is so that when the person cums/ejaculates, there is a place for the semen to go! If you stretch the condom tightly over the head of the penis, this will not only be uncomfortable, but also dangerous.

2. The condom was not stored properly. If the condom was near heat (in someone's back pocket, in the glove compartment of a car), the rubber weakens and makes it more likely that the condom will break. Condoms need to be kept in a cool (not cold) place. A nightstand, in a purse, or coat pocket are good places. Just make sure they stay away from sharp objects!

3. A fingernail tears the condom while it's being put on. File those nails and be careful! And no ripping open the condom package with your teeth. You could rip the condom that way too.

4. The wrong type of lubricant was used. Remember, only water-based lubricants should be used. Oil-based lubricants such as lotions, Vaseline, and massage oils should *not* be used on condoms. Oil eats through the rubber. Use water-based lubricants only, such as KY Jelly, Wett, Astroglide, and Cornhusker's Lotion.

By taking these condom-breaking reasons into consideration the next time you have safer sex, you will be having even safer "safer sex!"

Different Types of Condoms

Even if used correctly, all condoms are *not* the same. They come in different sizes, shapes, textures, and thicknesses. Some condoms are made of polyurethane and can be used if you or your partner is allergic to latex. Which condom is best for you? While I cannot answer that question, I have looked at several condom reviews from magazines such as *Men's Health*, *Men's Journal*, *Cosmopolitan*, and *Jane*, and also from websites such as www.condomania.com and www.drugstore.com. From these reviews, and from things I have learned elsewhere, I have come up with a few suggestions.

Size Can Matter

There are condoms that are snug fitting, condoms that are regular sized, and condoms that have extra room either all over, or just in the top, or "head." If a person has trouble cumming too soon, that person may want to try a snugger fitting condom. These condoms either say "snugger fit" on them, or most condoms made in Japan tend to have a snugger fit. Beyond 7 is another brand that is traditionally snugger.

Most people will want to get an average-sized condom. If you're not sure which kind to get, I would try a condom that does not say it's snug or has extra room. Then, once you try those out, you can go from there.

And yes, there are condoms that are bigger out there. But bigger is not always better. Unless you are really, truly, honestly someone who needs a bigger condom, I would not suggest getting one. A bigger condom can be baggy on someone, and that will cause it to feel bulkier and less sensitive. However, some people like the bagginess because they like the friction that goes along with it. Overall bigger condoms include Magnum and Trojan Supra. Condoms with more "headroom" include Inspiral and Maxx.

Thinner Is Better

Because all condoms have already passed strength tests, you can rest assured that any condom you buy will be strong enough, no matter how thin it feels. In general, Kimono Micro Thin has been rated as the most thin, sensitive, and heat transferring. This means it feels the most "natural" according to a bunch of these magazine ratings. Japanese condoms as a general rule are thinner than those made in America. Trojans have a reputation (and the magazine ratings to back it up) of being thicker and rubberier than most condoms. Lifestyles are somewhere in the middle.

Spermicide/Nonoxynol-9

There is some debate as to whether there is enough spermicide on a condom to really do any good. But it cannot hurt, unless you are allergic to it. If you want extra protection from an unwanted pregnancy, use a separate spermicide in either suppository, film, foam, or jelly form.

All Those Different Colors and Textures

These features are mostly for fun. Certainly color does not affect the condom itself, but it can make sex more entertaining and fun. From all the reviews I have read, all those different ribs, bumps, and other textures do not make much of a difference. The only way to know if you like them is to try them out yourself.

A word of warning, however: *watch out for condoms that say they are "novelty." These condoms do not protect you in any way.* These condoms are often found in bathroom vending machines at rest stops, clubs, and gas stations. Why they even make novelty condoms, I do not know. I personally think they are misleading and to some extent irresponsible on the part of manufacturers. A person goes out of his or her way to be protected, be responsible, by buying a condom, only to discover the condom used does not protect against STDs or an unwanted pregnancy. It's simply not fair to have to read the fine print in these situations. One of the "novelty-condom" culprits is the glow-in-the-dark condom. Most of these are totally useless when it comes to protecting yourself (unless all you need to do is find your partner's penis when the lights are off).

In sum . . .

> *How it works*—the semen gets trapped inside the condom, preventing semen and possible STDs from entering another person. The condom protects the person wearing it by acting as a coat or shield.

What makes it a good choice—it's cheap, easy to get a hold of, and pretty effective.

Why it might not be right for you—you or your partner may be allergic to the latex.

How to get it—pretty much any drugstore, convenience store, or grocery store will have them.

Cost—anywhere from free to $10 for a box of twelve.

Wait time until it works—as soon as the penis is erect, put it on and you are ready to go.

How well does it work—only 2 percent of women will get pregnant if they use condoms every time the right way after a year of sex. *If not used properly*, 12 percent of women will get pregnant if they use condoms every time after a year of sex.

What can go wrong—it can break or slip off. But by reading this section you found out how to avoid these problems as best as you can!

Diaphragm/Cervical Cap

The diaphragm and the cervical cap are both dome-shaped pieces of latex that fit inside the vagina and act as barriers to prevent sperm from getting near the egg so fertilization can never take place. The diaphragm is a larger device, as it fits over the opening of the vagina. The cervical cap is designed to fit more snugly, right over the cervix at the end of the vaginal opening, so it's smaller. Both of these birth control devices need to be prescribed by a doctor, as they come in different sizes and a woman needs to be fitted and sized to see which one is best for her. Usually, spermicide is used with a diaphragm or cervical cap to add extra protection from unwanted pregnancies. Note: You need to leave either of these devices in your body for at least six hours after sex to make sure the sperm do not survive and sneak on in after sex!

In sum . . . the diaphragm

How it works—holds spermicide close to the cervix to prevent sperm from getting through to the egg.

What makes it a good choice—it's easy to use, and can also help fight STDs to some extent because of the spermicide.

Why it might not be right for you—you may not feel comfortable reaching inside your body to put the diaphragm in. It may not fit well.

How to get it—your doctor helps find the right size and writes a prescription for it.

Cost—around $20.00, plus the cost of the clinic or doctor visit. The spermicide is less than $10.00 a tube and is good for several applications.

Wait time until it works—some people suggest using a backup method for the first few times to make sure it fits okay and does not fall out. It works right away, once you get the hang of putting it in and can be put in six hours in advance of having sex.

How well does it work—over 90 percent effective, with spermicide.

What can go wrong—the diaphragm can slip.

In sum . . . the cervical cap

How it works—fits snugly over the cervix to prevent sperm from getting through to the egg.

What makes it a good choice—it's easy to use, and can also help fight STDs to some extent because of the spermicide.

Why it might not be right for you—you may not feel comfortable reaching inside your body to put the cervical cap in. It may not fit well.

How to get it—your doctor helps find the right size and writes a prescription for it.

Cost—around $30.00, plus the cost of the clinic or doctor visit. The spermicide is less than $10.00 a tube and is good for several applications.

Wait time until it works—some people suggest using a backup method for the first few times to make sure it fits okay and does not fall out. It works right away, once you get the hang of putting it in and can be put in twenty-four hours in advance of having sex.

How well does it work—over 90 percent effective, with spermicide.

What can go wrong—the cervical cap can slip.

Spermicide

Spermicide works because it kills sperm. It comes in many different forms—jelly, foam, film (like little squares of wax paper), and little suppositories (pill-like things that are inserted into the vagina). Spermicides offer some protection against STDs, but really not enough to feel completely safe from diseases. Although it can be used alone as birth control, spermicide is usually used with a barrier such as a condom, diaphragm, or cervical cap in order to be most effective.

In sum . . .

How it works—kills sperm before it reaches the egg.
What makes it a good choice—it's easy to use, and is available in the drugstore.
Why it might not be right for you—it's not the most effective birth control method out there.
How to get it—Buy it at your local drugstore or online.
Cost—anywhere from $5.00–$10.00 depending on the type and how much you are getting at once.
Wait time until it works—it depends on the type you use. Some work right away, like the foam and jelly, while film and suppositories take about half an hour to expand to their full form.
How well does it work—over 80 percent effective, if used right. But for most, it's only about 70 percent effective.
What can go wrong—not enough spermicide is used, the couple does not wait long enough for the spermicide to work, some sperm simply gets by.

? Question:
What happens to spermicide after sex?
—Twenty-year-old female in Wisconsin

Answer:
After spermicide is inserted into the vagina, it gradually oozes out over the next day or so. It is not absorbed into the body.
Dr. X, *We're Talking* teen health website

More Than One Equals Twice the Fun

As implied above, for the best protection, using spermicide with a diaphragm, cervical cap, or even a condom provides more protection against both an unwanted pregnancy and STDs. And if you know you are more protected, you will be able to relax and enjoy the moment more. Preparing in advance for sex means being able to worry less about possible unwanted consequences.

HORMONAL METHODS: LESS "FUSS," LESS PROTECTION FROM STDs

Hormonal methods are only available for women (though scientists are working on hormonal methods for men as well). They work by preventing the woman from ovulating—some "trick" the body into believing it's pregnant, others simply prevent an egg from implanting or being made in the first place. Hormonal methods remain with the woman at all times—they are not just used when she is engaging in sexual intercourse. They also do nothing to prevent the spread of STDs. Therefore, hormonal methods are best used by females who are having sex often with only one faithful partner. Also, both members of the couple need to be STD-free, or they will continue to infect and reinfect one another until the cows come home (or someone dies).

IUD

An intra-uterine device (IUD) is a small plastic device that is placed all the way into the uterus (you cannot feel it in there). There are two kinds of IUDs. One has a band of copper around it and can stay inside the body for up to ten years. The other type has a small amount of the hormone progesterone, which increases its effectiveness and reduces side effects. This kind must be replaced every year.

Despite their initial appeal, IUDs are not recommended for teens. First, IUDs work best in women who have already been pregnant once; those who have not been pregnant before may find that their uterus is too small to hold the IUD in place. Even if a teen has been pregnant before, there is a higher risk of getting pelvic inflammatory disease when using the IUD, making it simply not worth it.

In sum . . .

How it works—no one is really quite sure. Some say that it upsets the environment in the uterus enough to make it unpleasant for the fertilized egg to implant and grow. Some say it affects the movement of the egg and sperm enough to prevent fertilization.

What makes it a good choice—once it's in you, it does its job without you having to pay much attention to it.

Why it might not be right for you—it may not fit well, especially if you have never been pregnant. It puts you at risk for pelvic inflammatory disease.

How to get it—a doctor would put it in for you. But, a doctor would most likely not let a teen get one because of the risks mentioned above.

Cost—around $350.00 including the doctor visit.

Wait time until it works—it works immediately.

How well does it work—about 98 percent effective.

What can go wrong—the IUD may not remain in place, making the woman at risk for pregnancy. The woman can get pelvic inflammatory disease.

Birth Control Pills

Birth control pills, or "the pill," is the most common form of birth control in the United States. Pills containing synthetic hormones (both estrogen and progestin) need to be taken once a day for twenty-one days in a row, followed by seven days of no pills, or seven days in which nonhormone-containing pills can be taken (most packs of pills give you these fake pills so that you stay in your routine of taking a pill every day). During these seven days of fake pill time, menstrual bleeding (your period) occurs.

It's important to take the pill every day at the same time in order for it to be most effective; this is why most women take it either right when they wake up or at night before they go to bed to help remind them. Setting a routine is the best way to remember to take the pill consistently.

In sum . . .

How it works—the synthetic hormones in the pills prevent a woman from ovulating and the sperm from traveling.

What makes it a good choice—it's private and convenient.

Why it might not be right for you—you may not be able to remember to take the pill at the same time every day. No protection against STDs.

How to get it—a doctor gives you a prescription, usually for a year. Then you need to go to the pharmacy every month to get refills.

Cost—depending on health insurance, anywhere from $10.00–$60.00 a month.

Wait time until it works—Two to four weeks, depending on the last time you have had your period. Most clinics will suggest using a backup method for a month just to be safe.

How well does it work—about 99 percent effective if you take it daily at the same time every day.

What can go wrong—you can forget to take it, making the chances of pregnancy increase significantly.

THINGS TO CONSIDER WHEN CHOOSING THE PILL

1. **Cost:** You will be responsible for paying for your birth control pills every month. Make sure you have the money to do it.
2. **Responsibility:** You need to remember to take your pill every day at about the same time for it to work effectively. If you are a forgetful person, the pill is probably not right for you.
3. **No smoking!** If you are a smoker, you should not take the pill. Smokers who are on the pill are at higher risk for heart disease.

A WOMAN AHEAD OF HER TIME

Margaret Sanger, a nurse living in America in the early 1900s, was one of the first people to fight for women's rights to birth control. Back in the 1900s, there were strict laws that banned birth control information and Sanger dedicated her life to fighting this censorship. In 1916, she opened the first birth control clinic and as a result was arrested and sent to prison. After her release, she continued the fight to create legal access to birth control. In 1939, she began the Birth Control Federation of America, which later became Planned Parenthood. In the 1950s, her efforts made it possible to find research funding for the first birth control pill.

? Question:

I have been on Ortho-Tricyclene (birth control pills) for about a year and a half. Does the effectiveness of the pill ever wear down?
—Twenty-two-year-old female in Virginia

Answer:

No it does not. Sometimes your cycles can vary after years on the same pill, but you never lose effectiveness as long as you take them on a regular basis.
No worries,
Dr. X, *We're Talking* teen health website

? Question:

What are the chances of getting pregnant while you are on your period and on birth control, considering that you don't take your birth control for the days you are menstruating?
—Eighteen-year-old female

Answer:

It's important to take the pills every day at the same time, or there is a chance of pregnancy. You should not get pregnant on the days you are not taking the pill because you are having a period (meaning that you ovulated before your period started), and although the sperm can live in your body several days, you will start taking the pills again, and should be protected.

If you have missed a period, you can do a home urine pregnancy test, which is the same as those done by physicians' laboratories. Test the urine from the first time you urinate in the morning, when the urine is the most concentrated and would have the most pregnancy hormone to detect (called HCG). You can do the test at least one day after your period has been late.
Great Question,
Dr. X, *We're Talking* teen health website

Depo-Provera

Depo-Provera is a shot that needs to be given by a doctor every twelve weeks (three months). The shot contains progestin, which prevents ovulation so there is no egg that

FLAKE OUT ONCE?

Don't want your period on a particular month? All is not lost when you are on the pill . . .

If you forget to take a pill, it's possible that you could become pregnant. If you forget to take one pill (in other words, miss one day), take it as soon as you remember and take your next pill at the usual time. If you miss two pills in a row, take two pills each day for two days and then go back to your regular schedule. If you forget three in a row, you are going to have to use a backup method and start a new package once you get your period again.

Also, being on the pill allows you to control when you get your period. If the vacation you have planned falls on the very same week that your period is supposed to come, simply do not take your "fake reminder" pills and immediately start your next pack. That way, you will not get your period at all that month. It's perfectly healthy to do this every once in a while.

can be fertilized. Therefore, a woman cannot get pregnant.

In sum . . .

How it works—the Depo-Provera shot injects progestin into a woman's body, which prevents pregnancy from occurring.

What makes it a good choice—it's private and provides worry-free birth control for months at a time.

Why it might not be right for you— Depo-Provera takes a few weeks to work, so it's not for the impatient. Also, a woman's period usually will change while using this shot. For

WHEN THE PILL IS NOT AS EFFECTIVE

There are certain medications, such as penicillin and other antibiotics, which make the pill either less effective or even ineffective. If you are given prescription medication because you are sick, tell your doctor you are on the pill so that she can make sure she warns you of any possible drug interactions.

Young women who do not use a hormonal method of contraception (the pill, Depo-Provera, the patch, or the ring) are four times more likely to become a school-aged mother.

115

some, their periods become nonexistent. For others, their periods get really heavy. There is spotting. Many women gain about five pounds. No protection against STDs. You have to go to the doctor every month for the shots.

How to get it—a doctor gives you the shot every time you have your period.

Cost—around $120.00 for the year. Pretty economical.

Wait time until it works—two to four weeks, depending on the last time you have had your period.

How well does it work—very well—over 99 percent effective.

What can go wrong—for some women, the side effects are too much to deal with.

?

Question:

How long does it take for your first Depo shot to be effective?
—Seventeen-year-old female

Answer:

Depo is *not* instantly effective. You should continue to use a barrier method contraception, like condoms, for the first month after the shot. After, that, if you get your shots when you should, then you will continue to be protected against pregnancy.

Remember, Depo-Provera alone will not protect you from sexually transmitted diseases (STD).

Dr. X, *We're Talking* teen health website

Other Hormonal Methods

In the past few years, two new hormonal methods have become available—the "patch" and the "ring." The patch looks like a bandage; a woman puts a new one on every week for three weeks and then doesn't wear one when she has her period. A woman puts the ring inside her vagina for three weeks. Then, she takes it out for her period and puts a new one in.

In sum . . .

How it works—the synthetic hormones prevent a
woman from ovulating and the sperm from getting
to the egg.

What makes it a good choice—it's private and
convenient.

Why it might not be right for you—you might not be able
to remember to put a new patch on or a new ring in.
No protection against STDs.

How to get it—a doctor gives you a prescription, usually
for a year. Then you need to go to the pharmacy to
get refills.

Cost—depending on health insurance, around $20–$35
for a month supply.

Wait time until it works—Most clinics will suggest using
a backup method for a month just to be safe.

How well does it work—very well, over 99 percent
effective.

What can go wrong—the patch might cause irritation.
Girls who smoke should not use the patch or ring
because they can cause blood clots.

SURGERY: ONCE IT'S DONE, IT'S DONE

It's possible to have surgery to make your body unable
to have children. This is called sterilization. There are
two different types of sterilization—one for males and
one for females. Although the procedure for males is
much easier than the one for females, more women than
men get sterilized.

Vasectomy (for Men)

In men, sterilization happens when a doctor cuts or clips
the vas deferens, which is the tube where sperm travel
down to mix in with the rest of the semen. Although it's
possible to have a vasectomy reversed, it should be

considered a permanent form of sterilization, as many things can go wrong during the reversal attempt.

In sum . . .

How it works—by preventing sperm from being mixed in the ejaculate, or "cum."

What makes it a good choice—if you are absolutely certain you never ever want to get someone pregnant. Not even if you decide to get married and have a family.

Why it might not be right for you—you *never ever ever ever* want to have children. Also, you need to be at least twenty-one years old in order to get one.

How to get it—since this is a surgical procedure, you need to go to the doctor's office.

Cost—anywhere from $250.00 to $1,000.00

Wait time until it works—it takes about fifteen to twenty ejaculations until all the sperm is emptied out.

How well does it work—after those fifteen to twenty ejaculations, it should work perfectly, but a follow-up visit is needed to make sure there are no sperm left in the ejaculate. In less than two in one thousand cases, the surgery is done incorrectly.

What can go wrong—nothing really, it's a simple procedure. Maybe a small infection will result, but nothing really to worry about.

Tubal Ligation (for Women)

Women are sterilized using a procedure called tubal ligation. The fallopian tubes are closed off so that the sperm cannot reach the egg. This surgery is a permanent solution to birth control and should only be considered if you never ever *ever* want to have children.

In sum . . .

How it works—by closing off the sperm's path to the egg.

What makes it a good choice—it's very effective, and you only have to do it once.

Why it might not be right for you—you will never be able to get pregnant once you have this surgery. Also, you need to be an adult in order to have this done.

How to get it—go to the hospital.

Cost—about $4,000.00

Wait time until it works—it's effective immediately, but recovery after surgery takes one to four weeks.

How well does it work—about one out of one hundred women become pregnant each year after sterilization.

What can go wrong—the tubes can reconnect themselves over time, making it possible for the sperm to reach the egg. There can be complications during surgery.

IS IT WORTH THE EFFORT?

Here is a list of all the different ways you can try to prevent pregnancy, along with how well they work.[4]

Percent of Gals Who Will Get Pregnant Using This Method

	If used correctly	If used with the usual amount of mistakes
Chance (doing nothing)	no such thing	85%
Abstinence	100%	21%
Withdrawal	4%	19%
Natural Family Planning	13%	20%
Condom	2%	18%
Diaphragm/Cervical Cap	6%	18%
IUD	1%	no such thing
Spermicide	5%	18%
Birth Control Pill	less than 1%	up to 10% if you forget to take it
Depo-Provera	less than 1%	less than 1%
Patch or Ring	less than 1%	less than 1%

EMERGENCY CONTRACEPTION— THE MORNING-AFTER PILL

Mistakes happen. The condom breaks, your diaphragm slips, or two people have sex without birth control for whatever reason. If the woman is concerned about getting pregnant, there is a solution called emergency contraception. Emergency contraception is a series of pills that are taken at two different times to provide the body with a short intense dose of hormones, upsetting the normal pattern of hormones in the woman's body. This hormonal imbalance will prevent a pregnancy from occurring if the first pill is taken within seventy-two hours (three days) of the act of unprotected sex (the second pill needs to be taken twelve hours later). The closer to the sex act the pills are taken, the more likely the pregnancy will be prevented.

If you are under 18, emergency contraception requires either a doctor's prescription or it might be available through a pharmacist depending on where you live (go to www.not-2-late.com to find out). If you are 18 or older, you can get emergency contraception at your local pharmacy unless it does not carry it.

Without using emergency contraception, 8 percent of women who have unprotected intercourse during the second or third week of their menstrual cycle will become pregnant. With emergency contraception, only 2 percent will become pregnant. Taking emergency contraception can be rather unpleasant, causing nausea and dizziness. But for most women, it's better to feel yucky for a couple of days than to risk being pregnant.

It's important to remember that emergency contraception is exactly what it says it is—it is something to be used in an *emergency*. If you are sexually active, you need to have a different form of birth control that you use regularly other than this. Taking emergency contraception often can be taxing on the body and the soul!

I Know What to Do, So Why Is It So Hard to Do What I Know Is Right?

If you have read this book up to here, you now know all the safer sex methods that are available to you. To recap, they are:

1. **Choosing not to have sex**
2. **Using a condom**
3. **Being monogamous, getting tested, then using another form of birth control in order to avoid an unwanted pregnancy (if necessary)**

Congratulations! You now know all there is to know about being safe—or do you? How many of you know someone who knows how to be safe, and wants to be safe, but for some reason is not being safe? There are a lot of people out there who "know better," but still end up in risky sexual situations. Some of those reasons are:

1. **Peer pressure**
2. **Partner pressure**
3. **Media pressure**
4. **Gender pressure**

Although there is no way a book could cover all of these pressures in depth, they are worth taking a look at and thinking about how they influence your life.[1]

PEER PRESSURE—FROM THE INSIDE

Most of us hear about peer pressure from our parents and health teachers. We learn that we should not bend under peer pressure, that we should just say no, and that if our

friends pressure us into doing something, then they are really not our friends. I think most of us can agree with those statements. I also think many of you would, rightfully so, defend your friends and say that your friends would never force you to do anything that you did not want to do. You can probably choose better friends than that. So does that mean that peer pressure does not exist?

No way.

The strongest type of peer pressure, oddly enough, *exists in your own mind*. What do I mean by that? Here are a few examples:

- You are at a slumber party and your friends are all exchanging stories about their boyfriends. They talk about what a good kisser this one guy is, and then how he really knows what to do to a gal "down there." Everyone is giggling and having a good time. Meanwhile, you get very quiet. You have never had a boyfriend, never mind actually kissed a guy or done anything else. You are suddenly convinced that the whole party is going to turn to you and ask you what you think about all of this. You feel like a loser and feel as if you are the only person in the whole world who at sixteen has never hooked up with anyone . . .

- You are in the locker room after a game. The rest of the gang is talking about who they have "done," and bragging about their sexual exploits. You and your girlfriend have talked about sex, but have decided to wait until you have been dating longer, or that you want to wait until summer to have sex, when things are less stressful. You care about each other and are happy with the decision. Yet you find yourself telling the team that you have had sex, and are even giving a few details about things that have never happened . . .

- You are in the locker room after gym class. Before gym, a lot of your friends had health class, where they talked about AIDS and safer sex. "And then they talked about oral sex," says one of the gals. "That is so sick—who would want to put their mouth on someone's dick?" It seems as though the rest of the locker room nods in agreement and disgust. You and your boyfriend (or heaven forbid, your

**girlfriend), have enjoyed giving each other oral sex safely
and responsibly. But now, for some reason, you feel dirty
about what you do and make a promise to yourself that you
will never do it again . . .**

All of the situations described above are a form of peer
pressure, but they are examples of internal peer pressure.
That is, no one is going directly up to you and saying that
you should or should not do something. Instead, indirectly,
your friends make you feel abnormal, or as though you are
doing something wrong. It's completely normal to want to
fit in, to want to contribute to a conversation. It's natural
to want to be liked, or at least agree with what your friends
are saying, especially if they are talking in a large group. It's
understandable that you would listen to your friends to
hear what are right and wrong things to do in a sexual
situation. When what you do does not match what people
are talking about, it's logical that you may worry—worry
that you are the only person in the world who has or has
not done a particular sexual act.

The thing to remember, however, is that sexual
experiences are very personal. There is no timeline for when
you should or should not do things. And, above all, it's not
a race to see who can be the most sexually active first.
guinea pigs have sex for the first time when they are only a
few days old. Does that mean that guinea pigs are the
pimp-daddy, bad-ass animals of the kingdom? Does that
mean that a three-day-old guinea pig is mature? Of course
not. On the other end of the spectrum, lions, the kings and
queens of the jungle, wait several years before having sex—
are they an immature species? And gorillas stay with one
partner for their entire lives—are they whipped? Hardly.

Now, I do not want to spend too much time comparing
your sexual decisions to those of animals, but the point is,
your decisions about your sexuality are exactly that—yours.
And your friends are not the ones who will live with the
decisions you make for the rest of your life. Only you and
your partner live with those. It's hard not to care about
fitting in, but try to take a step back and think—if I have

sex, if I decide not to have oral sex, or whatever—why am I deciding this? Is it for me, or is it so that I can feel more normal with my friends? If your reason has anything to do with friends, or acceptance, you may want to hold off on your decision a little longer.

PARTNER PRESSURE— DOING IT TO STAY TOGETHER

Unfortunately, I get many e-mails and posts from girls who say that their boyfriends are pressuring them to have sex (I also get some e-mails from boys who say their girlfriends are pressuring them to have sex, and those are just as unfortunate). Sometimes, this pressure is very real, and sometimes it's imagined. What I mean by imagined pressure is that sometimes a girl only thinks that her boyfriend is going to want sex soon—they have been dating for a few months, and the girl just assumes that her boyfriend is going to want sex, and starts to freak out. She has not heard anything directly from her boyfriend, but expects to any day and is writing in anticipation.

There is no secret here. If you are not ready to have sex, talk to your partner about it. Choose a time to talk to him or her other than when the lights are low and things are getting all sexy and romantic. Talk to your significant other with the lights and your clothes on, when the two of you can have a serious, undistracted, conversation. If your partner does not appreciate your wishes, leave that relationship. They do not respect you and your choices, and that sort of relationship will go nowhere. (For more communication tips, read chapter 9.) On the other hand, you may be surprised to learn that your partner is feeling the same way you are—your partner may also not want to rush your sexual relationship any faster than you do. But you won't really know that unless you ask.

Just remember—if your partner forces you to have sex, no matter how many times you have had sex before, no matter how drunk he or she is or you are, that person is attempting or committing rape. *Rape is never acceptable.* (Please see chapters 11 and 12 for more information on this situation.)

MEDIA BLITZ—DON'T THE MOVIES OR TV TALK ABOUT ANYTHING ELSE?

It's true—there is a lot of sex on television. Advertising agencies live by the motto "sex sells," talk shows lure us in with the not-so-secret tales of other people's sex lives, TV soaps and dramas are full of romance and betrayal, and sitcoms make sexual jokes all the time. But is hearing all these sexual references harmful? Maybe they actually do some good—by exposing people to sex, perhaps the media is doing us all a favor by normalizing a behavior that many are too embarrassed to talk about in public. There are as many opinions about sex on television as there are people. (For an interesting look at television now compared to the past see figure 8.1.)

To me, what tends to be troubling about all the sex on television is not necessarily the fact that it's there. The

Figure 8.1 Television Then and Now[2]

What was on television back in those days? What was still being censored? Read all about it—it's pretty surprising!

1950s

OK
On *I Love Lucy*, the first pregnant woman was featured

Still Not OK
Even though Lucy was pregnant, the word "pregnant" could not be said. Neither could "sex."

1960s

OK
Married couples could share a bed (before they had two single beds in one room).

Still Not OK
The woman had to show that she had a nightgown on, even under the covers. No nudity!

1970s

OK
"Racy" sitcoms were full of double meaning phrases. Cleavage galore!

Still Not OK
The words "breast" and "virgin" were censored on episodes of *M*A*S*H*

1980s

OK
Women's bare backs on *Miami Vice*; a man's bare butt on *L.A. Law*. Talk of sex and erections on *Roseanne*.

Still Not OK
You could say "making love" but not "having sex" or "doing it."

1990s

OK
Children born out of wedlock on *Murphy Brown*. Partial nudity on *NYPD Blue*.

Still Not OK
Condom ads. The "f" word.

TODAY:
Reality TV and scandalous talk shows are where it's at. The more shocking, the better. Jerry Springer brings on pregnant mistresses, 3-way couples, closet cross-dressers and a dominatrix (and that is all in one show)! At the time of this writing, *Dog Eat Dog* is about to broadcast a special playmate edition. People find husbands and wives during a television miniseries. Sexual serial killers are covered in depth on the news. It's all here in the 2000s, whether you want it to be or not.

trouble is the way in which television (and movies and advertising and magazines . . .) shows sexual relationships and talks about sex. For example, in one research study, three out of four teens felt that because "TV shows and movies make it seem normal for teenagers to have sex" teenagers are more likely to have sex.[3] What is shown on television should not influence a person's decision as to whether to have sex or not. That decision is too personal to have something as mass-programmed as a television show influence it.

But when you are bombarded with sexual jokes, sex talk, and scenes of people having sex, it's understandable that you could get the feeling that everyone out there is having exciting, invigorating, crazy sex but you. More than half of all television programs have some form of sexual reference. When people talk about sex on television, 81 percent of the time they are talking about their interest in having some form of sexual contact, or are talking about sex that has already happened. Compare that to the fact that only 2 percent of all sex talk on television is expert advice, or factual information, and you can see that learning about sex through television might not be the best idea in the world.[4]

The other thing that is weird about sex on television is that there is a lot of kissing, and a lot of sex, but little else. Television shows people passionately kissing, and then, if the interaction continues, people have sex. There is no intimate touching, no "foreplay"—just straight from kissing to sex. And are there consequences to sex on television? Heck, no! In the most extensive study of sex on television, researchers found that only 9 percent (that is less than one scene in ten) of all sexual scenes made any mention of the risks or negative

HAVEN'T WE MET BEFORE? DOES IT MATTER?

Why bother getting to know someone better before you have sex? In an analysis of scenes from television that showed people having sexual intercourse, here are the types of relationships that they had with each other:[5]

The people were in an established relationship	53%
The people had met before, but had no relationship	28%
The people had just met	10%
Can't tell from the scene	8%

In other words, almost half the time there is a sex scene on television, the couple is not in an established relationship. It seems that casual sex is just as common as sex in a caring relationship if you believe television standards.

ON TV, TEENS ARE SLIGHTLY MORE RESPONSIBLE THAN ADULTS

Even though only 9 percent of all sexual references on television talk about risks and responsibilities, when teens are involved, the numbers show a slightly better picture. When teens talk about sex or are engaged in sexual activity on television, the risks and responsibilities associated with sex are mentioned 18 percent of the time.[7] But even though that is twice as much good talk as adults on television engage in, it's still well under half of the time—less than one in five, to be precise.

consequences of sex—most of these references occurred in scenes where people were talking about sex that they had, not when people were actually having sex. And only 1 percent of the sex scenes on television showed the couples having any sexual patience.[6] That is, once they started getting undressed, they were going all the way.

So what sort of picture of sex do you get from television? One that makes it feel normal to have sex, without talking about the risks and responsibilities, and without engaging in any types of intimate touching beyond kissing. And the other message there is that once you start taking your clothes off, it means that you are going to have sex.

Maybe it's not such a good idea to learn about sex from what you see on television.

MEDIA SEX MYTHS

If sex in real life were like sex on television, here is what would and would not happen:

- Sex would last for hours and hours
- The guy would never lose his erection
- People would *always* moan and make lots of noise
- There would be no need to discuss condoms, never mind use them
- No one would get pregnant or contract an STD
- Your hair (and makeup) would look perfect when you were done having sex

Sex on TV is real? Yeah, right.

GENDER PRESSURE—BEING A BOY OR A GIRL IN A SEXUAL WORLD

It's pretty obvious that gender—whether you are male or female—is a big deal when it comes to romantic and sexual relationships. Many people think of gender as the main criterion for what they look for in a potential partner! Gender can override every other characteristic in a person when deciding whom to date. That is how important it is.

Gender is also important in considering how we view people as sexual beings. To illustrate this, I drew a circle (as shown in diagram 8.1) and divided it into four components: the top half is labeled "sex" and the bottom half is labeled "no sex." The left half is labeled "boys" and the right half is labeled "girls."

I also filled in some common names (see diagram 8.2) that we use to call the people who fall into these four categories (excuse my language!). I have chosen only some of the many labels available for each section of the circle. Feel free to think of others on your own. Notice how the words that we use to describe people can be pretty loaded with meaning— some meanings good, others bad. It's clear that not all the sections in the circle are treated equally. Boys who have sex are given positive labels, while girls who have sex and boys who do not have sex are given negative labels. Girls who do not have sex are sort of confused—some of the names they are called are negative, while others are more positive.

Diagram 8.1

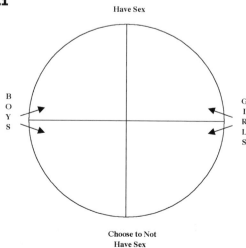

Have Sex

B
O
Y
S

G
I
R
L
S

Choose to Not
Have Sex

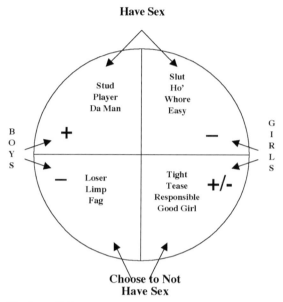

Diagram 8.2

What is pretty clear here is that this situation is hardly fair. No matter what girls do, have sex or not have sex, they can be called some pretty hurtful things. Even if a girl chooses not to have sex, she might be considered a responsible person, and at the same time a prude. But even being called Responsible or another supposedly positive name may not always seem so pleasant —it depends on who says it to her. If her parents call her a "Good Girl," that is seen as praise and approval. But if someone in her class rolls her eyes and says: "Anna? Hmph. She is *such* a Good Girl," the label takes on a completely different meaning.

And here is something else to think about—does a girl even have to have sex in order to be called "Slut" or "Whore." No way. All she has to do is strut a bit, or wear something just a little too tight, and she is considered to be sexual. And in this diagram, being sexual is a bad thing. Not natural, not normal, but awful—worthy of negative names.

Meanwhile, the boys seem to at least have a place to go. If they are sexual, they are called a number of names, all of which are positive, or can at least be made to be positive (even Players get a better reputation than Losers). But what boys can't do is freely choose between two options. With girls, even though they might be called a bad name no matter whether they choose to have or not to have sex, at least they can choose. With boys, their choices are taken away from them. Have sex, or be subjected to negative labels.

And that is not the only reason boys can't seem to win in this situation. Not only do boys lose their choices about what they can and cannot do, but the ways in which they can "earn" some of the more positive labels are usually by seriously endangering their health. Think about it. In order for a guy to

WOMEN IN MUSIC

Though girls and women who express themselves as sexual beings are often called "sluts," the one place where it's cool to be a slut—or at least a tease—seems to be in music. Think about Madonna who, in her early days, totally redefined female sex and sexuality with her crazy cone-bra outfits and songs "Like a Virgin" ("touched for the very first time") and "Papa Don't Preach" ("I'm keeping my baby"). And now look at Brittany Spears who made serious headlines with her risqué outfit on the MTV Music Awards. Sex appeal in music seems to be equated with how little the performer wears. And let's not forget Janet Jackson (the "Nasty Girl") and even lesser-known Sophie B. Hawkins (her one hit in 1992 was "Damn, I Wish I Was Your Lover") who defined herself as "omni-sexual," meaning that she was attracted to everyone!

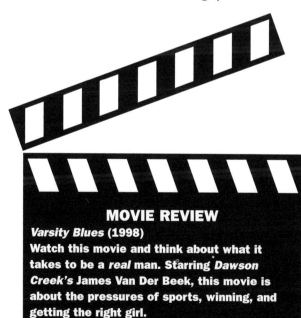

MOVIE REVIEW
Varsity Blues (1998)
Watch this movie and think about what it takes to be a *real* man. Starring *Dawson Creek's* James Van Der Beek, this movie is about the pressures of sports, winning, and getting the right girl.

earn a reputation as Stud or Da Man what else can he do besides have sex? Well, he can:

- ◎ **Fight**
- ◎ **Drink alcohol**
- ◎ **Use drugs**
- ◎ **Carry a gun**
- ◎ **Accept a challenge (like jumping off a high place, or racing his car)**

And simply doing these sorts of things is not even enough. He has to WIN at them. He needs to be better than the next guy. If he fights and loses, he is not Da Man, he is Loser. And if he has sex one weekend (he might be called Da Man by his friends, and get his high fives), his conversation with friends might look like this:

Guy 1: Hey—did you get some this weekend?
Guy 2: Yeah, you bet.
Guy 1: You da man!

But then next week, this happens:

Guy 1: Hey—did you get some this weekend?
Guy 2: Naw.
Guy 1: What happened?

Why should you have to explain yourself just because you had sex one week, but not the next? Or here is another scenario:

Guy 1: Hey Petey! Have you been gettin' any lately?
Guy 2: Boy, did I ever get some good lovin' last week. Feels nice just thinking about it.
Guy 1: Last week?!?!? I had sex three times just yesterday!

The moral of these stories is—if you work hard to be Da Man, you will end up being Da Loser because:

1. **There is always someone "better" than you—getting more dates, having more sex. Why bother entering a race you can't win? Besides—there are some things in life where**

quality is more important than quantity, and sex is certainly one of those.

2. Most of the things you need to do to earn such a title are downright dangerous. They could cost you your health, or even your life. Why risk your liver, brain, or genitals simply to be known as someone who parties a lot or gets plenty of action?

You just cannot win if you believe that being da man is an admirable goal. The pressure to live up to being Da Man is constant. You let up for one moment, and you get pushed right back down into the land of Da Loser. Rising above it all is the only way out.

?

Question:[8]
Are girls equally sexually active as boys are? It's said that a girl's sexual excitement is eighteen times more than that of a boy.
—Nineteen-year-old male

Answer:
Girls can certainly be as sexually active as the boys and are sometimes more interested in sex than their male peers. When it comes to sexual excitement or interest in sex this is very individual for both genders and it is difficult to make generalizations. Many people feel adolescent boys are more active sexually than the girls because they are more encouraged by the culture to be active and in general have more freedom from parental control.
Hope this helps,
Health Professional, *We're Talking* teen health website

GENDER AND CULTURE— ADDING FUEL TO THE FIRE

In addition to the names that society gives sexually active and nonsexually active boys and girls, people of color have additional stereotypes to deal with as they struggle to be seen as individuals, each with their own sexual identity. Most of these stereotypes are found in the media—movies, television shows, and music videos—but sometimes they come from the news and other places. African American boys and girls are seen in the media as troublemakers and highly sexually experienced for their age. Asian American girls are often seen as exotic and sexually objectified, while Asian American boys are rarely seen as having any sexual desires, instead being happier studying or working on science projects at home. Latinos are seen as sexist and macho, while Latinas are seen as pure and innocent, and often ultrafeminized. Native Americans, if they are mentioned at all, are either portrayed as victims or the perpetrators of violence, sexual or otherwise. Now, just by reading these I am sure you can tell that these generalizations are rarely, if ever, accurate. While it is true that one's background does help shape their thoughts and beliefs about sexuality, you cannot guess a person's attitudes about sex just by looking at the color of his or her skin. Religion, family income level, and life experiences all play a larger role in shaping one's sexual opinions than race. So, before you judge a person's sexual experiences by how they look, consider where your assumptions about his or her sexuality come from.

HOW BELIEVING IN THE NAMES PREVENTS SAFER SEX

Looking at the circle diagrams above, it's pretty clear that boys and girls are perceived differently. That is, people have different opinions of boys and girls when both are perceived to be sexually active. Because boys and girls are treated so differently, if they are perceived as sexually active, there is a wedge that separates the boys and the girls from each other, at a time when they should be close—the time when they choose to begin to be sexually involved with each other. This separation of the genders makes it really difficult to practice any of the three methods of safer sex. Think about it from the boys' point of view:

1. *Choosing not to have sex*—Can't do that, because then you fall into the category of Da Losers.

2. *Use a condom*—Can't do that, because what if you lose your erection? What if she changes her mind? Then you are back to being a Loser.

3. *Stay monogamous*—Yeah, right. What sort of Player stays chained to one woman?

And so, the boys are stuck. The girls aren't any better off practicing safer sex either though:

1. *Choosing not to have sex*—Do this, and you lose your man. Or, you are just stuck being called Tight, or a Tease.

2. *Use a condom*—If you bring it up, or heaven forbid have one, you might be called a Slut.

3. *Stay monogamous*—This seems like a good choice, but you have to talk about getting tested. And if you are tested, that means that you have slept around, and what does *that* say about you?

So, if you believe in all these labels and names, it becomes almost impossible to practice safer sex. Trouble is, these names and labels, and the beliefs about sex that are behind them, are all around you. So, don't feel bad if you use these labels and believe in them—it's hard not to. But trying to get out of this mind-set might be a good idea.

HOW THE HECK DO I THINK DIFFERENTLY FROM EVERYONE ELSE?

So what can each of you do to stop stereotyping people who are and are not sexually active? I am sure you can think of some ways on your own, but to give you a head start, here is a small list:

1. *Recognize that you live in a world of stereotypes.* By just recognizing the names we call people who do and do not have sex, you are well on your way to not thinking about people in such a limited manner. Being critical of this dynamic is one way to fight and challenge the stereotypes you grew up with.

2. ***Think about each person as an individual.*** **Each person has his or her own reasons for doing things. Every person and situation is unique. Remember that, and it becomes harder to call someone a name.**

3. ***Put yourself in another person's place.*** **Next time you think of someone as a Player, or Slut, or Loser, think about why you jump to that conclusion. What do you really know about this person? Are the rumors you hear true? And if they are, does that person really deserve that name?**

4. ***Stop using the names in the circle.*** **If you do not call people names, you are doing your part to stop the mentality of the circle.**

There is another really good reason to stop using the names in the circle. The more you use those names, the more you will believe them. And if you believe in them, you will use them on yourself. So, if you are a girl, and you think that girls who express their sexuality or have sex are sluts, when you feel sexy, you may think of yourself as a slut. As a result, instead of feeling good about yourself, you will feel like a horrible person. In the same way, if you are a boy and for whatever reason you do not want to have sex one day, you will believe you are a loser because if you truly were a stud, you would not give up the chance to "get some."

Believing in the words can only hurt you and those around you.

THE STORY OF THERESA

When Theresa went to school, not many people knew much about her. She kept to herself mostly, because her home was not a fun place to be. Her father said she was no good and that she would do her family proud if she just lost a bit of weight and conducted herself more like a lady. Her older brother called her an ugly bitch and laughed at her dreams to become a doctor—"Why would anyone want to be taken care of by someone as nasty and as dumb as you?" In order to avoid and forget what was going on at home, Theresa partied every weekend with an older crowd. At the parties, she got drunk early on in the evening (to sober up by curfew) and ended up hooking up with some random guy, going off to a bedroom. The guys at the party let this happen every week and hoped that the next time it would be their turn. Theresa is known to be "easy" and "good in bed," so the guys liked it when she was around, and told her that she was the life of the party. Then the rumors about Theresa started at school. The situation about her family life remained unknown, but her behavior at parties got out. Everyone in school started calling Theresa a "slut" and "ho." This of course made Theresa feel even more alone than when just her family was calling her names. So, when the weekend rolled around again, guess what she did? The same thing as last weekend. She got drunk, had sex with some guy, who on that particular evening would hold her and say nice things about her. It was the only time anyone said anything nice to her at all. That is how the vicious cycle of her unhealthy sexual behavior began and continued.

This is a true story. Today, Theresa is HIV positive and has herpes. She talks to classes about her life and how she would do things differently if she had the chance.[9]

IT HAPPENED TO ME: CAUGHT IN THE NAMES

Believing in the labels of sexually active boys and girls is easy to do. But, oftentimes, people who look at themselves in this light end up losing out on their sense of self-worth or their ability to be in a relationship. Read how believing in these names trip up both a girl and a boy as they talk about their relationship problems and ask yourself—if these two did not believe in the names, how might things have turned out differently for them?

Dr. Kris:[10]

Listen I need big advice. I had sexual intercourse with this guy who is like in love with me. Then about two weeks later I started dating this other guy while I was going out with the guy I had sex with. Then I cheated on both of them with this kid my friend hooked me up with. Then I told them both the truth and decided to stay with the guy my friend hooked me up with. The other guys won't let me go and don't understand that we are teenagers. I am fifteen and so is the guy I slept with. Now him and the other guy I cheated on are starting rumors about me. Do I sound like a SLUT? Please GIVE ME ADVICE . . .

Thank-you
Sincerely,
J. age 15

Dear Dr. Kris,

You probably don't get many letters from guys but I am in need!!

I have cheated on my girlfriend three times, well, not really cheated, but I kissed three different girls, and she is very mad and upset. She doesn't trust me any more, but I did those things when I wasn't sure about our relationship, and what I wanted out of it, but now I know that I don't want anything but her and being away from her is killing me. I want to be with her the rest of my life, but I think I have lost her and I don't want that . . . Please Help Me.

Those things with the other girls happened in the past and she just found out, what can I say to her? What do I do to show her that she can trust me again? I love her with all my heart and, I put her before I do myself. How can I show her I still care and want to be with her?

Please help me. I can't take being away from her any longer. I don't know what to do, I can't think, I can hardly sleep, my only goal is getting her back and I can't do it. I need help please, I'm desperate for her, I miss her, I love her, please help!!!!!

In need of my girl—please help me!!! Thank You,
B.

Communicating about Sex

9

The most important element of a great relationship and a healthy sex life is both simple and almost impossible at the same time. The secret ingredient is good communication. Talking about sex, your feelings, and your relationships is not easy. It makes you vulnerable, open to a lot of pain, and can be very embarrassing. But it can also lead to a very rewarding experience. Learning to express yourself to those you care about leads to self-confidence, the ability to be close to others, and a more complete life.

In order to communicate effectively you must: (1) know what you believe, (2) know what you want to say, (3) know when is a good time to say it, and (4) know how to say it.

KNOW WHAT YOU BELIEVE

You can't tell someone how you feel, what you want, or what you believe if you don't even know yourself. It's important to take time out for yourself to think about you and what you want. What are your values? What is important to you in a relationship? What are your sexual limits? Your sexual desires? What do you hope for your future? Knowing these things about yourself makes it possible to express them to others. It will still be difficult, but at least you know what the honest answer will be to these important questions.

KNOW WHAT YOU WANT TO SAY

We all know that it's a good idea to say some things and keep our mouths shut about others. For example, telling your best friend that you do not like her prom dress is probably not a good idea—especially if she already ripped the tags off or if it's the night of the big event. Why is this a good time to be silent about your opinions? Because it does no one any good to air it out. Your friend can't do anything about it, and she may feel insecure about how she looks because of it. Sharing this opinion will not make you feel any better either, so why bother with it? Keeping your thoughts to yourself in this instance is the best way to go.

However, there are times when it's best to say what you are thinking and how you are feeling. If you are in a relationship with someone, it's a good idea to tell that person what you are and are not comfortable with sexually and romantically. Without communicating these basic but very important points, a relationship cannot last.

There are mixed reviews about whether or not you should tell someone how you feel when you are not in a relationship with that person. If the person is showing signs of interest in you, then it might be a good idea to break the ice and confess some feelings. But if the person tends to shy away from you, then even if that person does return your feelings, they may not be ready to admit it for some reason. One word of advice—even if you believe you are madly in love with someone you do not have a relationship with, it's best to not spill all your feelings at once. Open up slowly, and give both of you a chance to get to know each other. Coming on too strong can scare a person who is surprised by your interest!

KNOW WHEN IS A GOOD TIME TO SAY IT

There are good times and bad times to bring up a conversation about sex and relationships. The best times to talk about serious things like being together or what does and does not feel good in the relationship either emotionally or sexually are times when both of you feel calm, happy, relaxed, and safe. In other words:

Good times are:

◎ **When the two of you are alone,**

◎ **When the sun is shining and you can take a walk together,**

◎ **When you are feeling good and secure about yourself.**

The not-so-good times to talk are when there is a lot of stuff getting in the way of a clear head. Neither of you is able to think clearly, and it's easy to not listen carefully or concentrate the way the topic of conversation deserves.

Bad times are:

- ◎ **When the two of you are hot and bothered sexually,**

- ◎ **Passing notes in class,**

- ◎ **If either or both of you are drunk or on something,**

- ◎ **When either of you is very angry or sad,**

- ◎ **When one of you has to leave for an important obligation in less than half an hour.**

Picking a good time to talk is just as important as knowing what to say. A person cannot respond to your thoughts and feelings if they are too distracted to hear them or you are too upset to express them coherently!

KNOW HOW TO SAY IT

Clear communication is a critical component of a healthy romantic and sexual life. When people offer and/or receive mixed signals, or are misinterpreted, they are placed at risk for unhealthy sexual consequences and actions. There are many different types of communication. An easy way to look at them is by thinking about ways we communicate with and without words. Here are some examples:

Communicating With Words	Communicating Without Words
Talking	Body language
Notes	Eye contact
Arguing	Touch
	Tone of voice

Oftentimes, these different ways of communicating contradict each other. For example, there may be a person who flirts with you all the time, puts his or her arm around you and all that, but then says no when you ask him or her out. Someone might say he or she cares about you, but then never makes eye contact with you or always has an excuse when you try to get together. This sort of mixed communication can be frustrating to a person who is trying to understand how another person truly feels about him or her. Therefore, it's important to talk about certain issues directly with that person if he or she appears confusing or contradictory. At the same time, you should also think about the ways you are communicating with someone and see if they are consistent or not. And if they are not consistent, try to do your best to change your ways of communicating so that they are consistent with your feelings.

For the most part, the best ways to communicate something you feel very strongly about are with words. No one is a mind reader—if we do not tell someone what is going on inside of our head, chances are they will not understand how we are feeling. When this happens, miscommunication is possible and there is a chance someone can get confused or even hurt over the situation. It's important to remember that people should make decisions about their relationship as a part of a couple.

ARE THESE TWO REALLY ON THE SAME PAGE?

Check out this story[2] written by a girl who can't tell what is going on in her romantic life. Given all the mixed messages, who can blame her?

Well at my school dance I went with my best friend Ron. So my friend Maria went with her boyfriend Jose. And well I dared them to kiss cuz they never do. So they did it and then Maria said I had to kiss Ron. And me and him looked at each other. He said, "Maria that's different cuz you two are going out. We are best friends." Well I did it cuz the only person Ron will listen to is me.

So then after that Maria and me ran away to talk. But when we would turn around there would be Jose or Ron. So I said, "You guys stop being hound dogs!" and they both stopped.

Well anyway I have asked Ron out lots of times and he has said no. Then the DJ started to play slow songs so Maria made me and Ron dance. Well we did and after that dance me and Ron were holding hands. Before I left the dance me and Ron hugged.

Does he really like me? I mean he has said no to me so many times. We talk on the phone every night. He knows my school schedule by heart. Basically he knows it better than I do. And I've never told him it. When me and Maria would switch coats at school he begged me not to switch coats. Cuz he didn't like going up to Maria in the halls.

He's not stalking me. But all I had to do at the dance was snap my fingers, and he would follow. I slapped him when we were slow dancing cuz he was drifting off into space, and he didn't care! Usually he would care, but he didn't. He won me a bunch of stuff.

Ron's sister hates me cuz she says I call to much and I said uh no its the other way around. He calls me I just return them. Today when I called him back he said his mom wouldn't let him pick up the phone. His mom doesn't let him talk to people on the phone cuz she thinks he is planning to bomb a school. I need to know does he like me or what? Or is he just obsessed with me?

My friend writes on my hand, "I ♥ Ron" everyday on my hand and he knows it. He knows how much I care and love him. But now I think he feels the same about me to.

NEGOTIATING STRATEGIES

There are times when communication needs to become a one-way conversation. If you believe your needs are not being heard or being met, or if you are feeling pressured to have sex or to go further than you want to go, it's helpful to know how to try to get out of the situation. Here are four ways to get yourself out of an unpleasant situation.

"Think It Over"

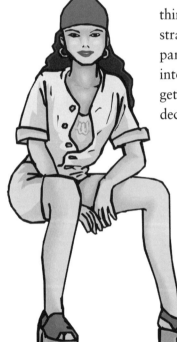

Thinking it over means telling someone you need to think about something first before you actually do it. This strategy is all about buying time for yourself and your partner. It can be used at anytime you are feeling pressured into an uncomfortable situation or sense you may be getting into a situation where you may be faced with a decision to have or not have unsafe sex.

"Think it over" phrases:

◎ **I'll call you back,**

◎ **I'll let you know by (specify day) if that's cool with me,**

◎ **I have to check with my parent first.**

Stay Strong

Staying strong means holding your ground when someone has heard your decision, but for some reason has chosen not to respect your words. When a person does not listen to or respect your limits, they are treating you unfairly and are not to be trusted. You are put in a position where you have to restate your feelings directly, clearly, and without room for debate. When this happens, it is time to restate your opinion loud and clear!

Stay strong strategies:

◎ **Use the person's name who doesn't seem to be listening to get their attention,**

◎ **Hold up your hand in a firm way and restate your message,**

◎ **Repeat what you said in a strong, loud voice and say, "I said . . ."**

Walk Away

You can walk away from a situation any time that you feel that talking isn't getting anywhere and you believe it's safe to leave. Sometimes you might want to talk about the situation first by either "thinking it over" or by "staying strong." But sometimes your partner will not listen and other times you might not think that it's worth it. This is when it may be best to just walk away from the situation.

Walking away strategies:

◎ **Get up and leave,**

◎ **Know where you are going,**

◎ **Pretend you are about to get sick and bolt.**

Get Help

There might be a time when you are going to need help to get out of a situation. Getting help—no matter who you are—whatever race, gender, age—is a great strategy to use in many situations.

Getting help phrases and strategies:

◎ **Yell "HELP!" (some people say to yell "Fire" to get attention)**

◎ **Yell, "Someone come over here,"**

◎ **Yell "Omigod! You gotta see this!"**

◎ **Call 911,**

◎ **Call a friend's name who might hear you,**

◎ **Make sure a friend knows where you are and who you are with at all times. Tell that friend that if you do not check in every hour or so to come look for you.**

BE HEARD!

TALKING WITH ADULTS

Talking with adults about sex and relationships can be a lot different from talking with them about other things. It can also be a lot different from talking to your friends or partner about sex. This is especially true if the adult in mind is a parent, or at least someone who is legally responsible for you.

The key to talking with your parents about relationships is to listen to what they have to say. True, you may feel as though your parent has no clue about what is going on in your life, or what things are like today, but parents do tend to have more life experience simply because they are older. Listening to what they have to say will get you some respect, show them you can be mature, and allow you to understand where they are coming from. You do not have to agree with their point of view necessarily, but giving them the opportunity to talk gives you a better chance of being heard in return.

If you disagree with a parent's expectations or wishes, talk to them about it. You may not "win" the argument, but expressing your opinion allows them to get to know you better and may help you get your way sometime in the future. Talk in a calm voice when the two of you have plenty of time to hash out the problem areas. This also helps show that you are getting older, more responsible, and mature enough to handle tougher decisions and bigger issues. Whining and yelling doesn't make a good impression, and nothing much gets accomplished (except maybe a fight) if an intense conversation feels rushed.

Different families react to talking about sex differently. Different parents allow for different levels of discussion and disagreement from their children. You probably have a good idea what you can and cannot say to a parent. But, when in doubt, try opening up to them. You may be surprised with the results. And, if they refuse to talk to you about sex, at least you know you tried.

Why It Might Be a Good Idea to Tell a Parent, or Other Adult

There are times where something happens to you, like an unwanted pregnancy, a painful breakup, or a sexual assault, when it's not a good idea to deal with the problem alone. While talking to a friend about it is a great idea, sometimes talking to an adult—especially a parent—is an even better idea. At first the mere thought of talking to a parent about heavy issues may sound crazy, but think about it—parents can:

- Sometimes have more power because they are legal adults.
- Like it or not, sometimes authority figures listen more closely to an older person. Getting an adult to represent you, or come along with you, can make your side of the story more believable and seem more urgent.
- Understand you in a way no one else can.
- A parent you have grown up with has known you your whole life. They may be able to understand what you are going through better than you think.
- Give you permission.
- In some states, you need parental permission to get an abortion. Sometimes you might need a parent's okay to use your health insurance.
- Be the only one who is there for you unconditionally.
- Talking to your parents about difficult issues will bring you closer together. At first there may be a lot of yelling and tension, but in the end, more often than not, going through a rough time brings people closer.

However, there are situations and times when going to a parent is not a good idea. In these cases, talking to another trusted adult or calling a hot line where adults have volunteered their time because they want to help teens in need can be just as good—or better—as going to a parent who is not capable of giving you the support you need.

? Question:[3]

How do I tell my mother I was molested? I don't want to lose her trust and I don't want to see her cry! Will she be mad at me?

—Sixteen-year-old female

Answer:

Almost always mothers want their daughters to come and tell them when they have been hurt in some way. If you ask your mother for some private time with you and tell her you need to talk something over she will most likely sense that you are serious and she will do it. If you truly think that she would respond poorly you could tell someone else, a relative, a school counselor, a doctor, or a minister, and have them be with you when you tell your mother.

Sometimes moms are very concerned and upset and rather than being able to listen and show they care they become tearful or angry. They may want to get back at the person who did it or because they are worried about you she might say something like "How could you let that happen?" Usually this initial shock passes and moms can be a great help. Tell your mom what YOU need: to be held, to be listened to, or whatever. Keeping your troubles all to yourself is the worst thing because even if you try to forget about it, it is likely to continue bothering you.

Hang in there and good luck,

Health Professional, *We're Talking* teen health website

10 Great Relationships

HUMANS NEED RELATIONSHIPS— BUT NOT *THAT* MUCH

Relationships are a very important part of human life. Healthy relationships help babies grow faster and stronger, help people have better self-esteem, and make communities safer places to live. One example that illustrates how people need human contact is an experiment that was conducted in the 1950s. Babies in an orphanage were raised in two different ways. The first group of babies were fed and bathed and clothed, but otherwise were raised in isolation in order to prevent them from catching any infectious diseases. Feeding took place in the crib with a propped-up bottle. There was little social give-and-take, little talk, little play.

The second group of babies was raised in a group setting where there was a lot more social stimulation. They were held when fed, attended to when they cried, and played with on occasion. After three or four months, the babies in these two groups began to differ from one another. The babies in the first group became withdrawn and expressionless. They rocked themselves, holding their bodies close to themselves. Some babies even got sick, even though they could find nothing wrong with them. From this study, researchers have concluded that people need human contact simply in order to survive.

But many people have taken the need for relationships to the extreme. They believe that they absolutely need to be in a relationship in order to be somebody, feel loved, or simply "fit in" with the rest of the world. In short, there are people out there who believe they are nothing without a boyfriend or girlfriend. Sure, being in a relationship may make you feel as though you belong, as though you are wanted, loved, and desired, but what does that say about you if you feel you are nothing without a someone?

Wanting to be in a relationship simply in order to feel better about yourself and your social standing has an effect on your relationship—a bad effect. The desire to be in a relationship just to improve social standing or in order to get into a "cooler" set of friends or in order to feel as though you belong will influence the expectations you have on your relationship. You may believe that simply being in a relationship will make you more popular, feel better about yourself, and make you more mature. A relationship cannot do all those things. Inevitably, such unrealistic expectations are not met and end up placing a strain on the true bond between two people. No matter whether you are in a relationship or not, you are still going to be you. Liking yourself outside the relationship is essential in order to have great friends and a great significant other.

REASONS TO LIKE SOMEONE

Out of all the different reasons a person would want to go out with another, there are two basic types of reasons. The first type of reason is a personal reason. Personal reasons are reasons that concern you and your partner only. There is no consideration of anyone else in your decision to date each other. If you are dating someone because you like them for who they are, the two of you get along well together, you like and respect each other, then you are dating for personal reasons.

The second type of reason to go out with someone is a social reason. Social reasons are reasons that consider other people and how they think about you or the person you are with. So, if you are dating someone just because they are popular, so that you will be invited to the "right" parties, or simply because you think only lame people do not date, then you are dating for social reasons.

Bottom line is that relationships are more successful if they happen for reasons that are personal to the people involved in the relationship and are not determined by social pressures.

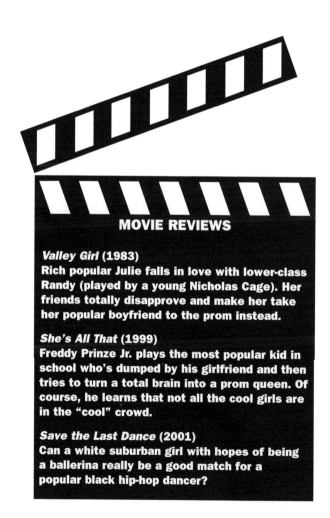

MOVIE REVIEWS

Valley Girl (1983)
Rich popular Julie falls in love with lower-class Randy (played by a young Nicholas Cage). Her friends totally disapprove and make her take her popular boyfriend to the prom instead.

She's All That (1999)
Freddy Prinze Jr. plays the most popular kid in school who's dumped by his girlfriend and then tries to turn a total brain into a prom queen. Of course, he learns that not all the cool girls are in the "cool" crowd.

Save the Last Dance (2001)
Can a white suburban girl with hopes of being a ballerina really be a good match for a popular black hip-hop dancer?

How can you tell if you are interested in being in a relationship for personal as opposed to social reasons? Do the following exercise and see!

Your Dream Comes True[3]
Okay, now I want you to imagine you can go out with anyone you want for a day. I mean anyone. Imagine you are with that person, and it's the most perfect day ever. You two have the best time possible. Get a good picture of that person and your day together. Imagine what you would do together (don't get too excited now . . .). You will always remember that day together as the most perfect day with this completely gorgeous, wonderful person. Picture the person that will be with you on your perfect date.

Now there is a catch to this perfect date (Of course! There is always a catch!). You can't tell anyone about it. And if you do try to tell someone—anyone—about it, no one would believe you. In fact, if you tried to tell anyone about it, you would be the laughingstock of your friends. How does the catch to the story make you feel? Does it change the person you want to be with? Why or why not?

Going through this imaginary exercise might help you figure out if you are more interested in dating a particular someone for personal or social reasons. If you were annoyed when you heard the catch to the story, or said to yourself, "Then what is the point of being with that person?" chances are you want to be with that person for *social* reasons. If you still choose the same person, despite the catch to this game, congratulations! You are probably choosing that person for *personal* reasons.

CRUSHES

What the heck is a crush anyway? At some point in time, most of us have had one. Or two. Or thirty-seven. We know it when we have one, but crushes are pretty hard to define. To me, having a crush on someone is falling in "love" or in "like" with someone you do not even know, or being attracted to someone without them knowing about your feelings. Getting a crush on someone is actually pretty easy— you don't even have to get to know the person before you have a crush on someone. I mean, how many people get crushes on celebrities and never even see them in real life? Not even from a distance? How often does a heart skip a beat when a beautiful person walks by, even though that gorgeous specimen is completely oblivious to the fact they are being watched? How many

times is a particular name scribbled on a piece of paper over and over again during a particularly boring class lecture? Yup—crushes are everywhere.

MOVIE REVIEW

Can't Hardly Wait (1998)
Preston is in love with Amanda (Jennifer Love Hewitt) the girl of his dreams since freshman year in junior high. But she doesn't know he exists. So, during a party he gives her a letter that he wrote and rewrote a million times in hopes that he can win her heart.

But even though *getting* a crush is easy, oftentimes *having* a crush is tough. Sure, it may be fun at first to see if you can "accidentally" run into your crush at school, or at the mall, or at a party. A simple smile from your crush can send you into utter bliss for hours. But, after a while, a crush can get pretty tiring and difficult. You want the person to know how you feel, but are paralyzed by the fear of rejection. The pain might start to eat away at your very soul. The obsession you have with this person may even start to interfere with friendships, schoolwork, or other activities. As soon as a crush starts to hurt, it has gone bad.

The reason crushes don't usually last long, and are not satisfying, is that they are not real relationships. Sure, the feelings that a person has when they have a crush on someone can be very real. But the relationship is not. First of all, there is often no relationship between these two people at all (take, for example, the celebrity crush—talk about someone not knowing you exist!). Second, the feelings that a person has when they have a crush on someone are not always based in reality. In fact, they are based not on an *actual* person, but on what that person believes their crush should be like, or wants them to be like. What I mean by this is, if you have a crush on someone, it's almost impossible to see that person as they really are—you put that person on a pedestal. A crush has no faults. A crush can do no wrong. A crush is a perfect specimen of a human being.

But crushes are people. And all people have faults. It's important to remember that. In fact, when someone has a crush on another, it's sometimes a good idea for that person to get to know their crush as much as possible. Learn about their good points, but also their not-so-good points. Know that they have faults, just like anyone else. Know that they are different from you. Know that they have different opinions, fashion style, and interests that you wish they had. By personalizing a crush, you put them back in their place—on earth where they belong.

Try saying "hi," try doing something together, even if it's just science lab or homework. Actually get to know the person behind the crush. If you still like that person—despite the fact that they do not and will not fit your idea of perfection—that's great. You may actually like a human being. If you don't, that's okay too. Seeing people as they are is the best way to have a good relationship with someone special—different, imperfect—but still special to you.

NOW THAT WE ARE TOGETHER, HOW DO WE MAKE IT LAST?

There is no secret formula that will guarantee a perfect relationship. No strict code to follow, no "to-do" list that will ensure relationship bliss forever. However, there are some important elements that, if not present in a relationship, may cause the bond to weaken instead of strengthen with time. Here are some things that are really important to creating a good relationship with someone. Remember—these things are not enough to keep a couple together, but without them, it's unlikely two people will stay together for very long.

WE'VE ALL BEEN HERE

DrG:[4]

I have a problem. I am really in love with this guy that goes to my school, but I don't think he even knows that I exist. I don't really talk to him and now that it's summer, I don't even see him at all. I wanna get to know him, at least become friends or something. I need to know how I can just go up to him and introduce myself. I know he knows my name and stuff, but he doesn't really know *me*. I have had the biggest crush on him for three *years*. I just want to know if he likes me. None of my friends know that I like him, so I've kinda kept this whole thing a really big secret. Should I tell one of my friends and then have them ask him if he likes me? I am afraid that he will say no. That he doesn't like me. That would totally shatter my heart. I need help please.

Ask yourself:

▶ Can this girl *really* like this guy if he doesn't really know her and he doesn't even know she exists?
▶ Can you actually know someone if you have never talked to that person?
▶ Can you like someone without even having spent any time together?

Components of a Great Relationship

Although every couple is different, there are a few basic characteristics that all good relationships should have. Briefly, they are:

Trust

Trust means that you believe in your partner, your relationship, and in the times you communicate with each

other. Trust allows each of you to have your own lives, be able to spend time apart, and have close relationships (not sexual ones) with other people—both boys and girls. If you believe in each other and the relationship, there will be less insecurities, worries, and jealousy between the two of you.

Respect

Respect means liking the person for who they truly are and what they do. It means being proud of that person and his or her personality, dreams, and accomplishments. The two of you feel privileged to be seen with one another—not just because of how popular each is, but because each thinks that the other is a great person who has a lot to offer everyone.

Balance and Compromise

A great couple spends quality time together and quality time apart. They encourage each other to engage in activities and hobbies that they like, even if the other person doesn't find them so interesting. Of course they also do some things together. It is important to share common interests, but it is just as important to have things that you do on your own so that each of you is a distinct person without the other.

Sometimes it is hard to balance your together activities with your solo activities. When that happens, the two of you need to talk to each other about what is really important to you. There may be times when you can't do everything you want to do because you need to take your partner's feelings and wishes into consideration. That's where compromise comes into the picture. Sometimes you need to give some of your time, and sometimes you simply need to say to the other that this activity is very important to you and you are willing to sacrifice a different event, but not this one. In a great relationship one person is not always the giver and the other the taker. Each needs to do a little of both.

Expressing and Listening

Great relationships involve great communication. If you are not sure how your partner is feeling, ask. If you are feeling particularly happy, sad, or mad about something, tell your partner. People are not mind readers. Ask each other how they are feeling, what matters to them, and if they are happy.

Work and Dedication

The bottom line is, a great relationship takes a lot of time, dedication, and work from both halves of the couple. Without this effort, a couple will begin to take things for granted until their relationship dissolves into nothing.

THINKING ABOUT YOUR RELATIONSHIP

When you start to think about the relationship you are in—whether it is or is not working out okay—here are some things to ponder as you try to put your finger on what it is that the two of you need to take the relationship to the next stage:

1. *Your partner.* Sounds pretty basic, but it's an essential part of your relationship. Do the two of you really like each other, or are you just attracted to each other? Is the person you are dating a nice person? Do you like his or her friends? Interests? If the two of you are not friends, the relationship will not get very far on attraction alone.

2. *Your involvement with each other.* How much time do the two of you spend with each other? How close are the two of you really? How close do you want to be? A serious relationship takes a lot of time and effort from both people.

3. *The nature of the relationship.* What do the two of you do together? Do you have fun? Truly enjoy each other's

company. It takes more than physical attraction and mutual friends to have a true relationship.

4. *Your feelings about and in the relationship.* How does the person you are with make you feel? Happy? Loved? Irritated? Frustrated? Good about yourself? Bad about yourself? In relationships there will always be tough times, but overall the good feelings need to outweigh the bad ones.

5. *The future of the relationship.* What do you want to get out of this relationship? A date to the prom? A wedding ring? A best friend? If both of you have very different goals for the relationship, that may make communication between the two of you difficult. If each of you wants something that the other does not, it may be best to move on. It's only fair to both of you to respect the needs of the other.

THINGS THAT CAN MAKE A GOOD RELATIONSHIP BAD

This is not where abuse and violence are discussed. For very important information on those topics, please check out the next two chapters on abusive relationships and rape. What we are talking about here are some things that can happen in any relationship that often make a shaky relationship take a turn for the worse. By acknowledging these feelings that you may have, you may be able to get through some rough times in a relationship.

Jealousy

Jealousy is being afraid that your partner is more interested in the person he is talking to than he is interested in you. Jealousy is being afraid that she will leave you if she becomes too interested in other activities that do not involve spending all your time together. Jealousy, according to *Webster's Dictionary*, is "painful suspicion of the faithfulness of husband, wife, or lover."[5] As the definition states, jealousy is pain and suspicion. Very little good can come of being jealous.

It's common to feel jealous in a relationship—especially a new one. You have not had time to get to know the person you are dating all that well, and you feel insecure about where the relationship is going and how much the person you are with really likes you. In fact, many psychologists believe that jealousy is a form of insecurity and is very natural. With time, you should feel less and less jealous in a relationship as the two of you grow closer and learn to trust each other.

If you find that your jealousy or the jealousy of your partner does not decrease with time, then there is a problem. If the two of you have been dating for a while, and there is still suspicion every time someone talks to a member of the opposite sex, then that shows there is a lack of trust in the relationship. Without trust, it's very hard to have a successful relationship.

However, there are times when you should not trust a partner or you learn something about your partner that makes you question your trust. If that happens, talk to your partner to get the situation resolved. What we are talking about here is those cases where the jealousy is not founded on realistic dangers to the relationship—it's all in the person's head and no matter what the other person does, the jealousy never goes away. If that is the case, then the jealous partner may need to figure out where those insecurities are coming from (talking things like this over with a counselor is helpful). Solving those sorts of insecurities isn't easy, but until a jealous person does, that person will continue to face those feelings in every relationship.

Betrayal

Back to *Webster's Dictionary*; to betray is to be false, deceive, prove faithless, or violate confidence.[6] In short, betrayal is lying and/or cheating on your partner. Unfortunately, it's common for teens to cheat on their partners—some studies report that cheating happens in about one in three college couples. But despite how common it may be, almost everyone says that cheating is not acceptable in a relationship. Surprisingly, there is an equal chance that the boy or the girl in a couple will cheat—even though the stereotype is that it's the guy who does the straying.

Many times the person who cheats feels bad, but that still does not mean it's okay to do. Not only does cheating hurt the relationship, but it can also put your partner at risk for STDs if you have sex with someone else and do not use protection. If you believe that you might cheat on your partner, talk to your partner about being less serious, or break off the relationship completely. If you think you are going to cheat, that is a sign that the relationship may be too serious for you, or that the two of you are growing apart. Relationships change over time, and most relationships do not last a lifetime. It's good for both of you to be honest up front about your feelings and maybe step back from the commitment. If you think you are being cheated on, talk to your partner about it. It will be a hard conversation to have, but in the long run, being honest with each other about the commitments you are and are not ready to make will make your relationships more successful.

Conflict

Before I get into this topic, let me make one thing perfectly clear: There is nothing wrong with conflict in a relationship. In fact, a little bit of conflict in a relationship is a good thing. Getting into an argument or debate with your dating partner shows that the two of you are being honest with each other and true to yourselves by sharing what you believe, even if those opinions do not match the beliefs of the other. It shows that the two of you, although wonderful together, also have your own thoughts and feelings—you are your own person without the other. When you feel close to someone, it's only natural that you are going to disagree with them from time to time, and that you two are going to do things that will make the other upset in some way. And because you care about each other, and care what the other thinks about you, it makes sense that when a disagreement happens, one or both of you might feel sad and upset. That's okay too, providing that the two of you work things out together.

And that's the catch here. A great relationship is not about *whether* a couple has conflict from time to time, but about *how* the couple deals with conflict when it comes up. The best way to deal with a conflict is to talk about it when both of you are not really upset. Of course, it's normal to feel sad, angry, or irritated with your partner when the two of you disagree. However, this is not the best time to talk about the problem. If the tension is too high, take a step back from the problem, or even from each other, and leave the issue alone for a while. Only when the two of you are both calm and ready to talk will you be able to address the problem rationally and productively. And when you do talk about it again, try to stay calm, really listen to your partner's side of the story, and work on an agreement that both of you thinks is okay. A little give-and-take can go a very long way.

There are many ways to end an argument that never work. They are:

1. *Violence.* **Never never never hurt someone when you are disagreeing over something. If you find yourself being hurt during an argument, leave immediately and go to a friend or relative you can trust. For more on this, see the next chapter.**

2. *Ignoring the problem.* **Sure, if one or both of you is really upset, you should forget about the argument—temporarily. But if you do not talk about what happened, the problem will keep coming up again and again until something is really done.**

3. *Doing all the giving or all the taking.* **Without truly listening to both sides of the argument and working out a compromise, someone's opinions get shut out. In a good relationship, two people need to work together to make things happen. If someone is always giving in to the other, that person is sacrificing too much of themselves just to have a partner.**

11 Abusive Relationships

DATING VIOLENCE AND ABUSIVE RELATIONSHIPS ARE EVERYWHERE

One out of every five teen girls will be in an abusive relationship.[1] Up to 68 percent of teens will experience some form of assault on a date.[2] Know the warning signs, know the facts, know your rights. Teen dating violence is a common occurrence and there are many ways to help yourself or a friend if you find that you are in a violent relationship or have experienced dating violence and you need help or support.

> **FACT**
>
> *No one*, I mean *absolutely no one* deserves to be the victim of sexual abuse or dating violence. You did not do anything to deserve an abusive relationship. You should not have "known better." Although many people do, do not blame yourself for what has happened. Seek support and live your life with respect.

ANYONE CAN BE A VICTIM

When we think about an abusive relationship, we usually think of a guy victimizing a girl. However, the reality is far from this assumption. For example, gay and lesbian couples sometimes abuse each other. Most of the time, same-sex couples do not abuse each other, just as most heterosexual couples do not abuse each other. But same-sex dating violence does occur, and like any other form of violence, should not be accepted.

Just like in heterosexual abuse, in same-sex abuse, one person tries to control the thoughts, beliefs, or conduct of their partner. They can control the person through abusing them emotionally, sexually, or physically. An additional form of emotional abuse for someone who is gay, lesbian,

163

or bisexual may be to "out" them (or threaten to out them) at school or to family or friends if their sexual orientation is a secret.

Boys, too, can be the victims of sexual violence in a heterosexual relationship, and they often are. Conservative estimates figure that one in five or six boys is sexually abused before the age of eighteen (usually by a member of his family). But boys also experience dating violence—the younger the boy in a dating relationship, the more likely he will experience dating violence.[3]

When a boy experiences abuse, he is unlikely to seek help from his parents or the police, or anyone. Even though it's important to get help if you are in an abusive relationship, it can be extra hard for a boy to admit he is being physically abused by a girl. After all, there are a lot of messages in society that tell us that boys are supposed to be stronger than girls, and that boys should be able to stand up for and protect themselves. Being a victim of abuse can make a guy feel embarrassed or weak. A boy might get hit by his girlfriend, but may not want to fight back, because he is afraid he might hurt her. Or maybe he simply thinks he is supposed to "tough it out." Boys can also be emotionally abused—an overly possessive or jealous girlfriend can isolate him from friends and after-school activities.

The truth is, abuse *can* happen to anyone, but it *shouldn't* happen to anyone. If you are a boy who is the victim of dating violence, you have every right to get out of the relationship and seek help as any girl should. If you are a gay or lesbian who is being abused or threatened by your partner, talk to a trusted adult or friend, or call an abuse hot line in your area (look in the phone book under "abuse" or "rape").

THERE ARE DIFFERENT KINDS OF DATING VIOLENCE

When we think of abuse, most of us think about someone hitting another. Although this behavior is certainly abusive, there are three different kinds of abuse: physical, emotional, and sexual.

Physical

Physical abuse is when a person causes bodily harm to another. Ways people are physically abused include:

◉ Being hit,

◉ Being punched,

◉ Having their hair pulled,

◉ Being burned with a cigarette,

◉ Being thrown out of a car,

◉ Having their fingers bent backward.

Emotional

Emotional abuse is when someone makes you feel insecure, meaningless, ugly, or afraid. They try to control you through words and actions instead of physical force. Ways people are emotionally abused include being:

◉ Called names like "stupid" or "whore" or "fat" or "weak,"

◉ Interrogated—even after they have told the truth—about where they have been and who they were with,

◉ Laughed at or humiliated in front of others,

◉ Accused of loving someone else or having an affair,

◉ Isolated from family and friends,

◉ Made to feel guilty about enjoying time apart.

Sexual

Sexual abuse is when someone does something sexually to you that you do not want. Ways people are sexually abused include:

◉ Being raped,

◉ Having their butt, breasts, or other personal part of their body grabbed or touched,

◉ Being called sexual names,

🌀 Being forced to have sex,

🌀 Having sex without protection even after they insisted on it.

One study reports that 3 percent of boys and 7 percent of girls in grades five through eight said they had been sexually abused. For grades nine through twelve, the numbers were 5 percent of boys and 12 percent of girls.[4]

THE WARNING SIGNS

Although there are many types of dating violence, there are patterns to look for if you think your partner may be abusive or may have the potential to be abusive. Ask yourself—does your partner . . .

🌀 *Act jealous and possessive toward you?* If someone will not let you see or talk to friends and family, if someone constantly follows you or asks you where you have been, that is abusive.

🌀 *Embarrass you by insulting you or calling you names?* They could do this in public or in private. Sometimes, when you ask them to stop, they will accuse you of having no sense of humor, taking things too seriously, or being too sensitive. Truth is, if you do not like what is happening, your partner should respect your wishes and stop doing it.

🌀 *Try to control you by giving orders and making all of the decisions?* If you offer an opinion, does your partner ignore it or say it's a dumb idea?

🌀 *Force you to do sexual things that you do not want to do?*

🌀 *Want to wrestle or pretend fight in a way that hurts you or makes you feel uncomfortable?* If you protest, does your partner say you have no sense of humor and are no fun?

🌀 *Hit, grab, or push you at any time?* It does not matter if the two of you are in an argument or not—physical violence is always wrong.

🌀 *Make you feel afraid that they might hit you if you make them mad or "do something wrong"?*

If you recognize any of these symptoms in your relationship, you are being abused. It is time to seek help. *If it feels scary, then it is abuse.*

HOW TO GET OUT OF AN ABUSIVE RELATIONSHIP

Getting out of an abusive relationship is not easy. It takes courage, support, and knowing what to do. If you are in an abusive relationship and want to leave your partner, here are some suggestions of what to do so that you are as safe as possible.

FREEDOM OF EXPRESSION?

There is constant debate among educators, people in the media, and fellow musicians as to whether rap music of the 1990s and today encourages violence toward women or if it is simply portraying a sad reality. Rap is full of lyrics describing black women as "bitches" and "whores," and male rappers often write about how many women they've raped and sometimes promote violence against women for "disobeying." Should rappers be responsible for the content of their music?

- *Tell people about your situation and experiences.* Talk to your friends, but also talk to an adult (or two) that you trust. Someone from your family, school, or church who you think will listen and believe you. Someone who will help you get out of a relationship that you no longer need in your life.

- *Avoid being alone.* If you are afraid that your partner will get mad and try to look for you to get you back, have someone with you at all times. If you cannot do this, call someone (even just to leave a message) about where you are going, what time it is, and how long you think it will take to get there. Then, call and let that person know you have arrived at your destination safely. It may sound like overkill, but you can never be too safe.

- *Document your experiences, and be as detailed as possible.* Write down what your partner did to you and when. Be as specific as possible. Give a copy of this writing to someone you trust. Your abusive partner may deny everything and this will help you prove you are right.

- *Do not meet your partner alone.* No matter how nice s/he is being, no matter how sorry this person seems, this person is controlling and manipulative. They will do anything and say anything to get you back. And the abuse will continue. Do not believe them—believe in yourself.

167

WHERE TO GO

The following websites are *great* resources for anyone who believes they are the victim of abuse:

- ◎ **For gay, lesbian, and bisexual relationships www.lambda. org/DV_background.htm**
- ◎ **For general teen dating violence www.ci.boulder.co.us/ police/prevention/teen_dating.htm**
- ◎ **If you suspect you may be abusive www.teenwire.com/ infocus/articles/if_19990917p016.asp**
- ◎ **Are you abusive in your relationship? www.teenwire.com/ warehous/articles/wh_20010727p114.asp**

FACT
It doesn't have to hurt physically to count as abuse. If it makes you feel uncomfortable, it is abuse.

Not near a computer? Here are some phone numbers to use anytime, anywhere:

- ◎ **1-800-838-8238 (for victims of domestic violence)**
- ◎ **1-800-442-4673 (Youth in Crisis hot line.)**
- ◎ **1-800-656-HOPE (National Sexual Assault Hotline)**

IF THE ABUSE IS TAKING PLACE IN YOUR FAMILY

Even though you are under their care, parents need to give their children a certain amount of privacy and respect. It's not okay for a parent to walk in on you when you are showering or changing (unless you say it's okay for that person to come in and they knock first). It's not okay for relatives to "experiment" sexually with each other when one or both of them are past puberty.

If you are being abused by a family member, talk to an adult outside the family about it. You can also go to a family member, but sometimes they will not want to believe you and even accuse you of making up stories. Family members will deny what is going on in the family if it's simply too hard for them to believe it. There is an agency that can help you if you cannot think of a person to talk to. If you are under the age of eighteen, you can call Child Protective Services in your area and talk with someone there about what is happening in your family. It's their job to make sure you grow up in a safe home that is free of abuse.

RECOVERY TAKES TIME

Getting out of an abusive relationship is not easy. Getting over an abusive relationship is even harder. But you can heal the emotional trauma and stress that most people get from experiencing abuse. The trick is, it's going to take a lot of help and support from others, and hard work on your part.

REMEMBER
You are *never* to blame for the abuse. Forgive yourself, and understand that what happened was not your fault. In time, you will be stronger.

First, give yourself time to get over the experiences you had. Do not compare yourself to others—everyone heals at their own pace. Talk to a counselor, or see if there are support groups in your area. Look for support groups online if you are in a rural area, or do not feel comfortable enough to talk about what happened in person. But in order to completely recover, most people need to talk to a professional eventually.

Know that some days will be harder to face than others. That's okay. Bad days may be triggered by something that reminds you of your past abusive relationship or by entering a new one too fast. Talk to your counselor or group about these times and your feelings. Don't try to get through this by yourself. It took more than one person to make the experience—it will take more than one to recover from it. In time, you will be able to have a happy, healthy life either by yourself or with a special someone who treats you with the respect that you have always deserved.

Rape

WHAT IS RAPE?

Rape is sexual intercourse that is forced or manipulated (that means, someone was tricked into having it). Although rape includes actions that are a lot like sex, rape is not sex. Rape is an act of violence. Rape is an unhealthy expression of power and dominance. Rape is illegal.

There are several types of rape. When a person is asked to make up a story about a rape, most will talk about a strange, evil person sneaking up on someone from behind a tree or the shadows of an alley. This type of rape is called *stranger rape*. Only 25 percent of all reported rapes are stranger rapes—that's one in four.[1] *Anyone can be raped.* Although most rape victims are female, boys and men can also be raped. Of male rape victims, 60 percent were assaulted before they were sixteen years old. As with women, most knew their attacker (86 percent). In only 13 percent of the cases was a woman involved in the attack.[2]

The more common type of rape is called *acquaintance rape*. Acquaintance rape happens between two people who know each other. Most reported rapes—75 percent—happen between two people who have met before. However, researchers believe that 94 percent of all rapes—reported or not—happen between two people who know each other.[3] If forced intercourse happens between two people who are dating, it's called *date rape*. If it happens between two people who are married, it's called *spousal rape* (even a married person has the right to say no and refuse sex). If it happens between two people who are related, the rape is called *familial rape*, a type of incest (if the rape happens to a family member under the age of eighteen, it's also child abuse and is subject to tougher laws). Date rape, spousal rape, and familial rape are all different types of acquaintance rape.

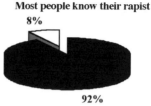

Most people know their rapist

8%

92%

% of rape survivors who said they:

■ **Knew their rapist**

□ **Did not know their rapist**

Acquaintance Rape[4]

The last type of rape is *statutory rape.* This type of rape happens if an adult has sex with someone under seventeen years old. Even if the sex is consensual (that is, both people agree to have sex with each other), it's still considered statutory rape. This is because the laws are written assuming that people under the age of seventeen are not able to realize the implications and importance that sex can have on a person's physical and emotional well-being. Therefore, the law was written to protect youth from being taken advantage of by older people.

Rape is sex without consent. A person must get permission from another before they engage in any form of sexual activity. Consent for sexual intercourse is when both people say yes. Silence—not hearing the word "no"—is not consent. Only a no-doubt-about-it "yes" is consent. A person has a right to say no at any time, even if they said "yes" at first. If they say "yes," then change their mind to "no," consent has been taken away. "No" does not mean "yes," or, "keep on trying until the person says yes." "No" means "no" and that is the end of it.

Another important thing to know about consent is that a person has to be aware of what is going on in order to give consent to sex. This means that a person cannot be:

- ◎ **Drunk**
- ◎ **Asleep**
- ◎ **Passed out**
- ◎ **On drugs**
- ◎ **Mentally or emotionally challenged**

and give consent. If someone has sex with a person under any of the conditions listed above, they can be tried for rape. Also, remember that if an adult has sex with someone under the age of seventeen (the exact age varies from state to state, and can even be as old as eighteen), that person has also committed rape.

People can say no to sex at any time. The following reasons do not justify unwanted sex:

- If a person dresses sexy;
- If a person is so turned on that they can't stop or help themselves;
- If a person has said yes to sex before—even if they have had sex before with that same person (even minutes before). A person can choose not to have sex with any person at any time, for whatever reason.

Unwanted sex is rape.

? Question:[5]
What percent of people have been raped?
—Sixteen-year-old female

Answer:
Rape Statistics (most of these statistics are from an April 23, 1992, report from the National Victim Center)

- In the United States, 1.3 women are raped every minute. That results in 78 rapes each hour, 1,872 rapes each day, 56,160 rapes each month, and 683,280 rapes each year.
- The United States has the world's highest rape rate of the countries that publish such statistics—four times higher than Germany, thirteen times higher than England, and twenty times higher than Japan.
- One out of every three American women will be sexually assaulted in her lifetime.
- One in seven women will be raped by her husband.
- Sixty-one percent of all rape cases are victims less than eighteen years old. Twenty-two percent are between the ages of eighteen and twenty-four.
- Seventy-eight percent of rape victims know the attacker.

◎ **In a survey of college women, 38 percent reported sexual victimization which met the legal definition of a rape or attempted rape, yet only one out of every twenty-five reported their assault to the police.**

◎ **One in four college women have either been raped or suffered attempted rape.**

If you have been a victim, please call 1-800-856-HOPE, which is a Confidential Sexual Assault Hotline, and talk to someone and get advice. Or visit the website at www.rainn.org/index.html
Hope this helps,
Dr. X, *We're Talking* teen health website

RAPE DRUGS

Rohypnol (Roofies, Rophies, Forget Pill) and GHB (Liquid X, Liquid E, Liquid Ecstasy) are two drugs that are used to help a person rape another. Both are illegal substances in the United States. It is extremely dangerous to use either of these drugs with alcohol. Mixing alcohol and either of these drugs can result in extremely low blood pressure, respiratory depression, difficulty breathing, coma, or even death.

Both Rohypnol, usually seen in a pill or powder form, and GHB, usually seen in liquid form, are colorless and odorless. This means that both of these drugs can be dissolved into a drink (alcoholic or not), and no one would be able to notice. If a person consumes a "dosed" drink, they will become drowsy, and may even lose consciousness. This allows the rapist to take advantage of his victim without the fear of them fighting back. In addition, as these drugs wear off, the person often cannot remember what happened to them, allowing the rapist to get away with the crime.

The best way to avoid being the victim of a drug-induced rape is to always be in control of your drink. Keep it with you at all times, and do not let a stranger give you a refill. If someone you do not know very well offers to buy you a drink, walk to the bar with that person, and watch the drink being poured yourself. Don't take a drink from a punch bowl. If you feel a lot more drunk or intoxicated than you believe you should given the amount of alcohol you have drunk, find a friend immediately and have that person watch you. Tell that person you may have been drugged, because you are feeling extremely "fuzzy," and are having a hard time remembering things; if you pass out, have that person take you to a hospital immediately, as the combination of these drugs and alcohol can be fatal. GHB is particularly dangerous because there is a very narrow margin between a dose that will produce intoxication effects and the amount that will lead to serious and harmful effects. Rohypnol can induce a coma and also cause death, so its effects also should not be taken lightly. Don't worry about the consequences of underage drinking—get your friend the help she needs. The price you may have to pay later is minor compared to the reality that your friend's life is in danger.

WHAT TO DO IF YOU ARE RAPED

First thing to remember is that it's *not* your fault. A rape is never the fault of the victim. Never, never, never.

Next, go to the safest place possible. Once you are safe, tell a person you can trust about what happened. This person may end up testifying in court for you if you choose to press charges. It will be hard to talk about what happened, but it's important. Hiding what happened will only make it harder to talk about later and you will only hurt yourself in the long run. It takes some people years to talk about their rape experiences. Talking about it as soon as it happened can help you understand that the rape was not your fault, and that it's crucial to get help right away.

Whatever you do, please do not bathe, shower, or wash yourself. You will want to, but it's important to resist cleaning yourself. This is because there may be small pieces of the rapist's clothing (like threads), or some of the rapist's semen or blood on you that can be valuable evidence. Place your clothes in a paper bag or wrap them in newspaper. Do not place them in a plastic bag, as plastic can destroy some evidence. Also, do not wash the clothes, as that will also get rid of evidence.

If you are hurt, immediately go to a doctor or hospital. You can call the police from there. If you are not hurt, call the police as soon as you can. The sooner a doctor examines you, the more chance there is of finding strong proof like blood or semen on your body, or on your clothes, from the person who attacked you. Bruises and cuts will stay on your body for a while, but semen, hair, and blood can be lost.

A doctor or special police surgeon will examine you after the rape. This examination may feel uncomfortable, but it's needed to collect any evidence on your body to help tell the story about what happened, and the doctor also needs to make sure that you are okay. The doctor will ask you about your sexual experiences, the last time you had your period, and your overall health. Then the doctor or a police officer will ask you about what happened during the rape. Even if you feel scared or ashamed, or anything else, try to remember as many details as possible. You can have a friend or a counselor in the room with you if you like.

The physical examination will also be difficult, but it's important to go through with it. The examiner will check inside your vagina for semen, bruising, and cuts. This is to not only collect evidence, but also to make sure you are okay. Your pubic hair will be combed, and your whole body will be checked for cuts and bruises. If you scratched or bit the rapist, tell the examiner. They will scrape under your fingernails and document any harm that you may have done to the rapist while protecting yourself (more evidence). Ask for the morning-after pill so that you do not get pregnant. Two weeks later, you should go to your regular doctor or clinic to get tested for STDs, including HIV. Three months later, go back and get tested for HIV again, and then another three months later, get tested for HIV one more time. You want to be safe and make sure that you did not get any STDs during the attack.

You will need to decide if you want to press charges or not. If you do not want to, that is okay. You will still go

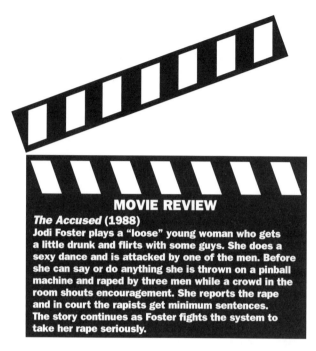

MOVIE REVIEW

The Accused (1988)
Jodi Foster plays a "loose" young woman who gets a little drunk and flirts with some guys. She does a sexy dance and is attacked by one of the men. Before she can say or do anything she is thrown on a pinball machine and raped by three men while a crowd in the room shouts encouragement. She reports the rape and in court the rapists get minimum sentences. The story continues as Foster fights the system to take her rape seriously.

through the medical examination, but you can tell the police officer that you do not want to press charges. They still need to report and record the rape, so they will put it in a casebook. If you do want to press charges, you can do so at any time, though the sooner after the rape, the better (for the sake of collecting evidence).

Reporting a Rape

Many of you may have heard about the anguish of prosecuting a rapist. Many may have heard the myth that a person should not bother pressing charges against a rapist because they are just going to go free anyway. While there is unfortunately some truth to these statements, you should know that the laws and punishments against rapists are getting tougher these days.

A study by the National Center for Policy Analysis (NCPA) shows that the number of forcible rapes decreased by 8 percent from 1998 to 1999 (the most recent statistics we have).[6] They believe rape cases have gone down because the punishment for rapists has gone up. Since 1980, the expected sentence for a rapist has tripled, and today more rapes lead to jail time than just a few years ago. However, the American legal system still has a long way to go when it comes to punishing rapists: all told, only 16.3 percent of reported rapes see the perpetrator go to jail.[7]

Rapes are the most unreported crimes. That means that more rapes go unreported than any other crime in America. It is estimated that two-thirds of all rapes are not reported to the police. There are many reasons that rapes are not reported:

- The victim does not want to talk about what happened to anyone,
- The victim fears that she will not be believed,
- The victim fears that the emotional trauma of the trial is not worth it, even if the rapist is punished,
- The victim fears that the rapist will hurt her further if she says what happens,
- The victim knows the rapist and does not want to get him in trouble.

All of these reasons make sense and do not make sense at the same time. Some of you may think that a crime should be reported, no matter what. Others may feel that the legal system cannot be trusted, and therefore don't see why it makes any sense to report a rape. The bottom line is: it's up to the person who was raped to make the choice. That person, if she decides to press charges, should get support from the legal system, her friends, and her family.

PREVENTING RAPE

It is never the fault of the victim if she is raped. However, there are things you can do in order to make it less likely that you will be a victim of a sexual assault:

- Do not walk alone,
- Always go to and leave parties with a friend,
- At parties, have a "buddy system," where every hour or half hour you check in with your friend to see how they are doing,

- ◎ Let other people know where you are going and what time you are expected at your next location,
- ◎ Watch how much you drink (or, ideally, avoid drinking altogether),
- ◎ Think about the level of intimacy you are willing to have with a person, and clearly set those limits out loud before things get hot and heavy,
- ◎ Be aware of your surroundings at all times.

If, despite being as cautious as possible, someone tries to rape you, consider the following:

- ◎ Yell "fire," or "police"; people respond to these words more than a cry of "help."
- ◎ If you run, run toward people or a public place. Run toward light.

GETTING HELP

If you or someone you know has experienced a rape, no matter how long ago, there are many places to turn for help and support.

- ▶ Rape, Abuse and Incest National Network (www.rainn.org; 1-800.656.HOPE) offers free, confidential counseling and support twenty-four hours a day, from anywhere in the country.
- ▶ Your phone book will have places to call under "Rape Services" in the yellow pages.
- ▶ Talk to an adult or close, mature friend that you trust. Getting help is the best thing you can do for yourself, but try not to do it alone.

MOVIE REVIEW

Girls Town (1996)
Nikki, a high school senior, commits suicide right after she and her best friend Emma talk about how much they are going to miss each other in college. After going through her diary, Emma learns that Nikki had been raped. The rest of the friends bond together, share their experiences with violence, and learn to move on after the loss of their friend.

WHAT TO DO IF A FRIEND IS RAPED

- Believe her words and her feelings,
- Be patient: It will take your friend a long time to recover from this event,
- Listen to her and be there for her,
- Understand that it's ultimately her choice as to whether to get help or report the rape. Support her in whatever she decides. She needs you now.
- Get support for yourself if you are scared, feeling alone, or angry (calling a hot line or talking to a counselor might help).

Other Important Topics

13

I have learned many things being an online sex and relationship advisor. One of the most important things I have realized is that many people have many questions about sex and relationships that are not covered under the more traditional topics in a book or sex education class. Here, I talk about some of the more popular, hidden topics to help you understand that they are not so weird, uncommon, or unimportant.

BODY IMAGE

Sex and your body are very connected. After all, most times (unless you are engaging in phone sex or cybersex or something like that) your body plays a huge role in a sexual encounter. So, it makes sense that thinking about sex will make you think about your body.

The bummer is, a lot of people do not like their bodies. This is especially true for girls, but there are a lot of guys out there who don't like their bodies either. The rates of eating disorders, diets, and steroid use in teens show how much young people are unhappy with how they look. Up to 20 percent—that is one in five—of high school girls throw up their meals as a way of controlling the amount of calories they consume at some point in their lives.[1] About 5 percent of all boys use steroids to change the look of their bodies.[2] A survey of high school students found that 44 percent of the girls and 20 percent of the boys were trying to lose weight—28 percent of the boys were trying to gain weight.[3] Only 5 percent of American women have *never* been on a diet in their lives.[4] Why are so many people unhappy with the way they look?

181

There is this crazy notion out there that only beautiful people have sex or are worthy of sex. That only attractive people are sexual people. This is simply not true. Humans are sexual beings. That means every person is a sexual being. But, it's easy to think otherwise, and that means that if we do not see ourselves as good-looking or attractive, then we might also think that we are not worthy of having a sexual or romantic relationship with another person. So, what happens quite often is that teens try to change their bodies—through dieting, starving, taking steroids, or overexercising—in the hopes that they will become more attractive and therefore be more likely to have a sexual partner.

A great place to get stats on eating disorders and body image is www. about-face.org. This site is famous for showing pictures of ads in magazines that make it easy to see why so many Americans are insecure about their bodies!

While it's true that most people like others who take care of themselves (you know, people who bathe, comb their hair, wash their face, etc.), there is a huge variety of tastes when it comes to attractiveness. There are people who like super skinny folks, and there are those who prefer a person who is rounder, bulkier, or has more curves. Some people go gaga over strong arms, while others see a well-manicured hand as the biggest turn-on. Bottom line is, no matter how much you change your body to make it fit an ideal, there will be people out there who do not think you are attractive. And, no matter what your body looks like, as long as you take care of what you have, there are people out there who will find you appealing.

There is another connection between sex and body image. The more you are comfortable with your body, the more pleasant and healthy your sexual experiences will be. If you are overly concerned about whether you think your partner thinks you look good, or if you wince if your partner grabs you by your "extra chunky" middle to give you a kiss, it's hard to enjoy the time you are spending together. It helps to have a positive body image in order to have a healthy sexual or romantic relationship. Otherwise, you will be freaking out over what your partner thinks about you, and thus be distracted from the tasks at hand. Relax, enjoy the moment. Nobody and no body is perfect.

OLDER GUYS, YOUNGER GIRLS

If you are a girl, you know the drill—you meet a guy and the two of you really start to hit it off. The two of you seem to have so much in common, and your friends think he is great. You want to tell your mother about him, but you do not dare for one simple reason: He is older than you.

Your mother and father would freak if they knew how old he is. You can hear their voices "Older guys are only after one thing. . . ." Well, how right are your folks? Here are some stats about girls who date older guys.[6]

- ◎ Girls with older boyfriends are more likely to experience pressure to have sex.

- ◎ They are more likely to have been forced to have sex when they didn't want to.

- ◎ They are more likely to have had sexual intercourse under the influence of alcohol and/or drugs.

- ◎ Having a partner five or more years older is associated with less condom and other contraception use.

- ◎ About one in five infants born to unmarried minors are fathered by men five or more years older than the mother.

- ◎ Teens with older partners are more likely to become pregnant than those who date partners who are similar in age. Teens who date older guys are also less likely to get an abortion.

RECENT RESEARCH

There are many studies that show a relationship between dating and weight concerns in junior high girls. Here are a few findings:

- ▶ Girls that are dating are more likely to be dieting and have disordered eating.
- ▶ Girls who are more sexually involved are more likely to have disordered eating habits.
- ▶ Bulimic girls have more dating partners and are more likely to get sexually involved earlier than girls who are not diagnosed with an eating disorder.
- ▶ Girls who believe popularity is important are more likely to think that thinner girls are more attractive.
- ▶ Girls who do not practice birth control and girls who are less likely to take control in a sexual situation are more likely to believe that thin is beautiful.
- ▶ Girls who believe that boys should be in charge on a date are more likely to be concerned about their weight.
- ▶ In other words, girls who start dating and being sexual early (that is, those girls that start dating and being sexual in junior high) are more likely to diet and be concerned about their weight than girls who wait until later in life.[5]

Not great things to hear. And these studies lead us to ask a logical question: If dating older guys seems like a bad idea according to both our parents and the research, why does it happen so often? There are many possible reasons. Girls mature faster than guys, so when a girl dates an older guy, she may be dating someone who has a similar level of maturity. Also, there can be a certain status associated with dating an older guy. He may have a job, and thus be able to buy more things for his girl. He might have a car, which allows the couple more independence. He may even have his own place, which means it's easier for the couple to be alone together.

But an older boyfriend has another side. He might have more power over his girl and may use this power to get what he wants. By buying her things or giving her a place to stay, he may expect sex in return. He may make the girl feel that since he is older, he is more sexually experienced (and needy), so he gets to call the shots on where and when they have sex, and whether they use birth control. The bottom line is, status and power are not cool if they are held over people. If someone wants to control you, that is not a good relationship to be in.

If you are dating someone older, think about why you are dating this person. Then, think about why they are dating you. If control and power are a large part of the picture, it may be time to reconsider what you are doing. Ask your friends—the ones you really trust—what they think. They'll tell you if the way your boyfriend and you act is more like father/daughter or brother/sister or boss/worker than they think is right.

THE VOICES OF THOSE WHO KNOW

How do you know if a relationship is right? Listen to yourself—you probably have the answer. If you feel deep down that something is wrong with the relationship you are in, then something is wrong with that relationship. You have to feel comfortable dating who you are dating. If you are not, then the relationship is not right. Also, if you have to lie about your age to be in a relationship, that is not a good start to the partnership. Without honesty, a relationship will not go very far. The truth is bound to come out! Be true to yourself first, and if the relationship is right, it will hold strong.

Dr. Kris,[7]
O.K. I really need help. I told this guy that I'm fifteen when I am only thirteen (and he is sixteen) and . . . he wants to have sex with me! . . . but I don't want to end up with a baby or AIDS or something like that. I really love him a lot. Please help me and tell me what I should do!

Dr. Kris,
I met this guy that is seventeen and I am fourteen. He says that he likes me and all, and I like him. Should I go for it or wait a little?

Dr. Kris,
I have a problem. I met this guy . . . He's funny and nice to talk to. There's only one problem—he's three years older than me and my mum forbids me to date anyone more than two years older than me.

Take time out to think about why a twenty-five-year-old man would want to date a fifteen-year-old girl. If the reasons seem shaky to you, that is because they are shaky.

ALTERNATIVE SEXUAL BEHAVIORS

Alternative sexual behaviors are things people do to turn themselves on that are not considered traditional sex. Sex in and of itself is a forbidden topic to discuss—when you discover that a certain sexual practice is labeled "alternative" it becomes next to impossible to find reliable information about it. Thinking about and learning about alternative sexual behaviors does not make you abnormal or a freak. Even discovering that you like some of them does not mean that someone is going to lock you up anytime soon. As with everything, alternative sexual behaviors done in a safe, consensual (meaning, both people agree to it), and responsible matter do not have to be bad. Read on to learn more.

Porn

From a definition standpoint, porn is short for pornography, which is anything that is created to cause sexual excitement or arousal. But when most of us think about porn, we tend to think about nudie magazines (*Playboy*, *Penthouse*, etc.), erotic fiction, and X-rated movies. Now, for the most part, these materials cannot be rented or purchased by people younger than eighteen years old. Adults have made

FACT
It is illegal for a person under eighteen years of age to pose for a pornographic movie, magazine, or Internet site.

these laws to protect minors from explicit sexual content. But the reality is, it's quite common for people under eighteen to have seen, or at least seen ads, for porn.

Making it illegal for a minor to own porn does two things: it can make it more desirable for a minor to own porn, and it makes porn seem like a very "dirty" and evil thing. There is some truth to this latter statement: Not all porn is created equal; there are levels of intensity when it comes to porn, and these levels have a lot to do with how they potentially influence the behaviors of those who use it. When porn is depicted using violent images, like rape, forced sex, or bondage, studies have shown that this can make people more violent in their own relationships and lives in general.

But it's not just violent porn that can influence a person's real-life sex life. Porn can both help and hinder a person's sexual health. Some ways that porn can benefit a person are:

- It can help them fantasize about what they might like or not like.
- It can be a safe visual aid for when people masturbate.

However, there are ways in which porn can harm a person's sexual health:

- It can interfere with that person's desire to have a real relationship.
- It can create expectations that real-life sex is actually like the sex that is in the movies or written about. The sex in these books and movies is exaggerated, as are the reactions of the people (they are *acting*, remember!). Real-life sex rarely lasts as long or is as exciting and "all that" as it appears in the media.
- All the bad and messy parts about sex are magically missing from porn. No one ever loses an erection, gets a headache, or falls off a bed by accident in porn. And, it looks as though porn stars are always in the mood for sex. But no one, I mean no one, is always in the mood for sex. Don't expect that attitude from your partner, or yourself.
- It can cause people to have unrealistic expectations about what they and others look like naked. Breasts, penises, and other sexual body parts are not as big on most people as they are on porn stars.
- In porn, safer sex is rarely mentioned. Where are the condoms and the concerns about pregnancy and STDs? Get real!

But the answer to the question many of you have, "Is it okay to like porn?" cannot be answered in a book. It has to be answered by you. Whether you want to make pornography a part of your life is a decision only you can make (mind you, it is illegal for stores to sell porn to anyone under eighteen years old). Some people like all types of pornography, some people do not like any form of pornography. Some people are okay with certain types or various levels of intensity. The bottom line is, do what you feel comfortable doing, and make sure anyone else involved is comfortable too.

Fetishes

The term "fetish" is often misunderstood and used improperly. A fetish, in medical and psychological terms, is an object that someone *needs* in order to get sexually aroused. The object actually *takes the place of* a human in terms of sexual feelings and interactions. A person who has a true fetish is not able to have a sexual relationship with another human being. A person who has a true fetish should talk to a counselor or doctor about getting help so that they can have healthy relationships with people, not things.

What most people think of when they think of fetishes are really "turn-ons." There are as many turn-ons out there as there are people. Some of the more common ones are high heels, leather, a certain color hair, or a certain occupation (nurse, police officer, etc.). For the most part, these sexual turn-ons and preferences are a private matter that you may choose to share with a serious sexual partner. Or, you may decide to keep them completely to yourself. Be careful about sharing them with any random person—they can, and will, be used against you for humor. Many people find anything even remotely sexual funny. If they find out that you are sexually aroused by anything that does not fit under their own definition of sexy, it becomes some form of psychological ammo to use on you. In truth, one person's turn-on is another person's turnoff, and there is nothing inherently wrong with that.

187

Shaving

Looking at photos of naked women (in pornographic magazines, for example), one could easily think that all women shave their pubic hair. This is simply not true. While most women in America do shave their armpits and legs (they do not in many other countries), shaved pubic hair is not nearly as common. In fact, it's pretty darn rare. If you do, however, decide to shave your pubic hair, you should do it for you—not because someone says you should. After all, it's your hair that is going to itch like crazy when it grows back (and it does too—I've asked around).

Multiple Partners/Sharing/Threesomes

I know I am supposed to be writing about how you should be making your own sexual decisions, but in this case I will make an exception. My advice to you is: Do not engage in a threesome. These sorts of relationships and sexual experiences can only end in a big mess of confusion, hurt feelings, and destroyed relationships. Sure, they may seem like fun in your fantasy world, but that is where they should stay—in the fantasy world. In porn movies, they look fun and sensual, but those situations are carefully choreographed and rehearsed, so that when you watch them, no one is feeling left out of the action or concerned about what is happening to them when their concentration is on someone else. Also, the people in these movies do not have to hang out with each other the next day. They just collect their paychecks and carry on with their lives. No mess, no confusion, no reality.

Power Relationships

There are all sorts of relationships that fall under this category. A parent–child relationship has some power issues that go along with it, as does a boss–employee relationship. What "power relationships" means in a sex ed book is sexual relationships that have an unequal power status. Fantasy and role play (when people pretend to be people they are not, or pretend to be in a place they are not) is often, but not always, involved. A lot of people will talk about BDSM, or "B&D" and "S&M." In these abbreviations, B = bondage, D = discipline, S = sadism, and M = masochism.

Bondage is when people are restrained with ropes or something else during sexual activity. Discipline is when strict rules are set in a sexual relationship, and punishment is administered when these rules are violated. Sadism is feeling sexual pleasure in hurting someone, and masochism is feeling sexual pleasure when one receives that pain. As with threesomes, or group sex, I again urge you not to engage in any type of sexual power relationship. The logistics of this sort of power relationship are very complex and the activities can be very dangerous if done by people who do not know exactly what they are doing.

ONLINE FLIRTING AND DATING

Chat rooms, instant messages, message boards, e-mails. These are the ways that you can communicate with another person online. And if you can communicate with someone online, you can flirt and develop relationships with people online. On one level, online interaction seems harmless and simply a great way to meet people. However, there are many things to consider as you develop relationships with other people online.

Safety Concerns

It's popular, it's common, but it's still potentially dangerous. Meeting people online has its good points and its not-so-good points. The good points are easy to spot—you can meet people that you otherwise would never run into, as geography is no longer an obstacle. You can meet people from your own town, so you do not have to worry about getting a ride or borrowing a car, or someone from a faraway location that you always wanted to visit. You can meet people with similar interests quite easily; all you have to do is go to a website that talks about things that you like, and *bingo*!—people who have your same interests are right there along with you. So, those are the good points. Let's go over the bad.

- ◎ No matter what a person tells you online, you have to remember that they may be lying. Even if you chat and write to this person for months, they may not be who they say they are. Even if the two of you start an online romance of sorts, it might be based on untruths. It's a harsh reality, but a possibility. You never know when a 5'5" female redhead you meet online could actually be a 6'3" guy.

- ◎ Don't give out personal information online such as your last name, phone number, where you live, or even your private e-mail address. People can use this information to find you, and their intentions might not be honorable.

- ◎ Be suspicious of those who want to know too much. Just as if you were meeting someone in person for the first time, there are certain things that are very personal that you would probably not talk about right away. People who ask personal details very soon should make you suspect their motivation for talking to you. Trust your instincts; if someone is making you feel uncomfortable, leave.

- ◎ It's almost a contradiction, but also be wary of people who tell you practically nothing about themselves after the two of you have been chatting for a while (weeks, months). People who never want to talk about themselves are probably hiding something, like their true identity, or another relationship.

- ◎ *If you do decide to meet someone in person that you have only known online, meet that person in a public place.* And, ideally, you should also bring a friend or two along. If this person really wants to meet you as much as you want to meet them, they will understand and respect your wishes to be safe. Encourage your online friend to bring some of his or her friends along too, to make it a group meeting. If they object, that is your cue to walk away. Also, let another friend or even your parents know where you are going. That way, if something happens, someone knows where you were last seen and who you were supposedly with. There is no reason to think this is overkill. Meeting someone in person that you only knew online is just like going on a blind date. As much as you would like to think you do, you might not really know who this person is and if you can trust them.

Having a Relationship with Someone Online

You have somehow beaten the odds and have met a person online that you actually like and want to date. In fact, the two of you have even talked about being in a serious relationship. So, what does this all mean? Here are some things to consider about online relationships:

- The person on the other side of the keyboard may be lying. Until you actually meet face-to-face, you honestly do not know who that person really is. Be careful about falling for someone that you have never even met in person.

- Online relationships tend to move a lot faster than relationships in real life. Why this is, I am not exactly sure, but I have some ideas. Part of the reason is the fact that you can spill your guts more easily on a keyboard than if you are looking someone in the eye: Typing "I love you" into cyberspace is a lot easier than saying it to someone. There is less risk, less chance of being hurt. It's also easier to say "I love you too" back when it simply is not true. Another reason online relationships move so fast is that it's easy for each person to fill in the blanks about the other person in ways that are perfect. Each person in the relationship can build up expectations, sometimes ones that are unrealistic, because it's easier to read between the lines online than deny the flaws of a person that is actually in front of you. You find your perfect match online because you can help create that person in your head.

- What is your level of commitment to someone you meet online? If you have an online boyfriend or girlfriend, is it okay to flirt with someone at your school? Can you go on a date with someone from your neighborhood? Can you have another online romance? People's feelings can get hurt if you do not talk about what is and is not okay.

- It's really easy to be dumped online, so be careful about being hurt. Love is always risky, but it's even riskier online. It is very easy for people to simply stop emailing and even

close their account. They don't have to look you in the eye when they pull the plug on your relationship. And when that happens, you are left alone with a lot of questions and no way to get them answered. People who do this are total cowards, but they're out there.

Cybersex

Cybersex is when you type out the sexual behaviors you would like to do with someone and they do the same back to you. Two (or more) people engage in cybersex either through instant messages, private chat rooms, or via e-mail.

Having cybersex may not seem like such a big deal—after all, you can't get someone pregnant or get an STD from it. But, after engaging in cybersex, some people feel strange about it. Sometimes cybersex can feel like the real thing. A person can get so involved in what they are doing that they believe what they are doing is real. They may regret doing it, may not be sure if it means they now have an actual romantic relationship with someone online, or could simply be confused about their feelings toward sex, their emotions, and this person.

So, my advice to you about cybersex is treat it like real sex. If you do not know the person, do not have cybersex with them in the same way that you would not have sex with someone you do not know in real life. Only have cybersex with someone with whom you would have actual sex. So many people teach you to respect your body when it comes to sex. But, you should also learn to respect your heart and your mind. Your heart and mind are just as involved—if not *more* involved—in sex than your body is. Therefore, seriously consider how you are going to think and feel after you have cybersex before you do it.

BREAKING UP IS HARD TO DO

It doesn't matter if you do the breaking up or you are broken up with, ending a relationship stinks. Of course, how you feel might depend on which end of the stick you are on, but then again, it might not matter at all. You will feel some or all of the following: sadness, despair, anger, relief, thoughtful, self-doubt, vengeful, strong, weak, alone. It's okay to feel all of these feelings at different times, and even all at once. The key to getting through a breakup is this: No matter how bad it hurts, sucks, overwhelms, or takes over your every thought, *it will get better*. You will hear many people say that, and you might not believe them, and might even get mad at people who say that. But it's true. After a breakup, people get better; they heal, and move on when they are ready. Note, I said when they are ready. It may take some time, and it *will* take some help from friends, relatives, good music, and maybe a counselor, but people survive breakups every day, and so will you.

To help you through that nasty breakup time, here is a list of Do's and Don'ts to consider:

DO	Write a hate letter or love letter, letting your recent ex know exactly how you feel.
DON'T	Send it. Burn it (along with some white sage for a cleansing of the spirit) as a symbolic end to the relationship. Have a friend witness the burning and make it a celebration of sorts.
DO	Express the emotions you feel.
DON'T	Lash out at your ex, your friends, your pet, or yourself. Beat a pillow, take a walk, talk to someone, let yourself cry instead.
DO	Grieve.
DON'T	Grieve 24/7. Give yourself a set block of time every day (MAX of thirty minutes) to obsess and think and wonder about what went wrong. But when that time is over, so is thinking about that relationship until the next day.

DO	Feel hurt, if that is how you feel.
DON'T	Hurt yourself. If you start to hurt yourself or even feel like you want to hurt yourself, call a suicide hot line right away. Or, you can also talk to a counselor or other crisis hot line. There are people out there who want to help you and want you around the way you are.
DO	Think evil thoughts.
DON'T	Act on them. Think about how bad it would be tomorrow if you did.
DO	Talk to your friends about how you feel.
DON'T	Make your breakup the only thing you talk about. Remember the rest of the cool things that you are all about? Talk about those things too! It will make you and your friends feel better and have a better time with each other.
DO	Be nice to each other.
DON'T	Try to stay friends right away. Allow for some time apart, to get used to the idea that you are no longer a couple. Being friends right away can be confusing and can be extra painful too. Chill out for a while. In time, the two of you will be able to spend time together again and it will not be totally strange.
DO	Take the time and think about what you learned from the relationship. Think about what was good about it and how it helped change you and make you more mature.
DON'T	Beat yourself up about what you shoulda or coulda done. There were many things your ex also coulda or shoulda done to make it work.
DON'T	Completely blame yourself or your ex for what happened. There are no faults here. The relationship did not work out, and that is okay. Now, learn from it, remember it, and move on.

LOSING SOMEONE YOU LOVE

Not all separations happen on purpose. Sometimes tragedy causes a relationship to end when no one is ready:

Dr. Kris,

My name is Jonatha, and I am a freshman in community college majoring in something, it was nursing, but now, who knows? Anyway, I guess that I am supposed to write to you about my love problems. Well, that's the thing . . . I don't have any. I haven't been in a serious relationship in two years.

My ex boyfriend and I were serious for five years. He passed away in a car accident two years ago. It was rough for the longest time. I was supposed to sit next to him at graduation, but he wasn't there. We were supposed to be king and queen of the prom, he wasn't there.

I need to get back into the dating game. I am hoping that you could help me.

Hi Jonatha:

I am so sorry to hear about what has happened to you. I have lost close friends to tragedy, but never a partner, so I can only imagine what it's like.

The first few things you need to do involve you and only you. You have to be honest with yourself about whether you are ready to date again. On one level, two years is a long time. On another, it is less than half the time you two were together. If you really want to start dating other people, that is fine. But I hope you are not feeling as though you want to date again simply because you feel you should.

Another thing to do is talk to a counselor (does your school have any for free or lower rates?) about your desires to date again. That person can help you set reasonable goals to get you back on your feet and looking around.

There is no time as to when you need to move on, but if you want to, that is great. Just remember that you have every right to be sad and grieve when you want, and that it is never too long ago to miss someone.

Dr. Kris

SEXUAL ORIENTATION

There are a lot of people out there who simply don't have sexual feelings toward people of the other gender. They either have feelings for people of the same gender, or they have feelings for people of both genders. In fact, about one in ten teens says that s/he is either attracted to the same sex, both sexes, or is not sure.

At this time, we do not know what "causes" different people to have different attractions to others. There is a lot of research out there, but no sure answers. What we do know for certain is that in our society, it's not easy to be gay, lesbian, or bisexual. There are many biases against people who consider themselves to be something other than heterosexual. These biases and the fears that go along with them are sometimes called homophobia—the fear of homosexuals. Homophobia can show up in many forms:

◎ **Name calling,**

◎ **Not wanting to be friends with someone who is gay,**

◎ **Having people think you are different and strange, even mentally screwed up,**

◎ **Being beaten,**

◎ **Being kicked out of your own home.**

None of these homophobic behaviors are right. If you believe that you are the victim of homophobia, get in touch with someone who will be your ally and friend. If you do not feel as though there is someone in town whom you can rely on, try talking to someone at PFLAG (Parents and Friends of Lesbians and Gays). PFLAG is a national organization whose mission is to "promote the health and well-being of gay, lesbian, bisexual and transgendered persons, their families and friends." To find the location closest to you visit www.pflag.org. A great place to learn more is www.youthresource.com, a directory for all gay, lesbian, bisexual, transgender teens and their allies!

LAWS AGAINST SEX

Texas, Kansas, Oklahoma, and Missouri currently outlaw homosexual sex. Idaho, Utah, Michigan, Virginia, North Carolina, South Carolina, Louisiana, Arkansas, Mississippi, and Florida outlaw oral and anal sex between both homosexual and heterosexual people![8]

This Closet Is Awfully Cozy, but I Want to Start Living!

If you believe that you are not heterosexual, you may be thinking about coming out to friends and/or family. Deciding to reveal your sexual orientation to others is a pretty big deal—it can be a very scary time. You may not be sure whether to make the big move or not. You are putting yourself on the line, making yourself vulnerable, and possibly opening yourself up to rejection from those who simply do not understand your sexual preferences. Here are some things to think about whether it's a good idea to come out or not:

SAD, BUT TRUE

Of teens who say they are either gay, lesbian, or bisexual:

▶ **42 percent say that they are teased or called names**
▶ **13 percent are abused physically in some way**
▶ **14 percent say that they feel unsafe at school because of their sexual orientation.**[9]

◎ *Make sure you have an ally.* Even if that person is an online buddy (from a trusted place like PFLAG—Parents and Friends of Lesbians and Gays), knowing you have someone you can talk to about the experience will help you feel strong.

◎ *Be comfortable being gay.* People might ask a lot of questions if you come out to them. The more sure of yourself you are, the more people will accept who you are. The more informed you are, the better you can educate them about your experiences.

FACT
One in five gay or lesbian teens has told no one about their sexual orientation.[10]

◎ *Who do you want to come out to*? How accepting do you think this person will be? How much control do they have over you? It's not a pleasant thought, but be honest with yourself. If you come out, do you think you will be kicked out of your home? Get a bad grade? Lose a friend? If so, don't blame yourself. Instead, feel sorry for the person who would react that way, but you might want to stay quiet.

◎ *Set aside a time to talk to the person.* Being in a calm quiet mood will help a lot when talking to someone as serious as this. Trying to rush this conversation will only make things more tense than they need to be.

◎ *Be prepared for any reaction.* The person might be angry, confused, surprised, upset, or a combination of feelings. They may act hurtful at first, then come around once the initial shock is over.

◎ *Remember you are you.* Let friends and family know that even though you are gay, that you are still the same person you have always been, with the same interests, feelings, and life.

◎ *Crush those rumors!* Try not to let people you care about find out about your sexual orientation through someone other than yourself. Be the first one to tell them; it lets them know that you are open and honest, and you do not believe your life is something to hide.

◎ *Never feel pressured to come out.* It's your choice and your choice alone. Come out only when you're ready and you want to.

MOVIE REVIEW
But I'm a Cheerleader (1999)
A popular cheerleader Megan (Natasha Lyonne) is feared to be lesbian by her parents so she is shipped off to a camp designed to set her "straight." There, she meets other gay and lesbian teens who struggle with accepting their sexual identity when everyone else wants them to just act "normal."

I'm Not Gay, but I Want to Be a Source of Support and Understanding

The experiences of gay, lesbian, and bisexual teens are often ones filled with loneliness, fear, and stigmatization (being left out). There are not a lot of role models out there for people who are questioning their sexuality. Simply being a friend that can be trusted, remembering that no matter which gender you fall in love with it can hurt just as much, and offering an undying friendship are great ways to help anyone feel accepted.

Also, don't tolerate name-calling. Challenge people who use words like "fag" and "queer" in an unflattering manner. And if you see a classmate being bullied because of their sexual orientation—whether it's known or just assumed—talk to a teacher or administrator about it. Such actions should not be tolerated by anyone. If you see a teacher ignoring (or even encouraging) any form of homophobic behavior, let the principal know. If you are still being ignored, put your complaint in writing and send the letter to both the principal and the school board.

INTERRACIAL DATING

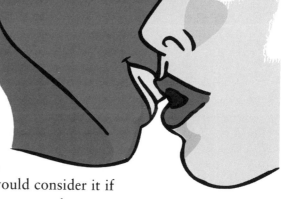

The topic of interracial dating is a concern for some couples. They are worried about what their friends think, what their parents think, and what society thinks. Well, there is good news and bad news. Good news is, for the most part, your peers support interracial dating. In one survey, 57 percent of teens reported having dated someone of another race, while another 30 percent hadn't, but would consider it if the right person came along.[11] Another survey of teens found that 80 percent of teens knew at least one interracial couple and over half (58 percent) felt that interracial dating was pretty common in their school.[12]

However, it seems as though parents and society are less accepting of interracial couples. One in three parents says s/he is not cool with the idea of his or her child dating someone from another race.[13] A major poll of Americans found that 68 percent of people believe there is discrimination against interracial couples, and 40 percent of people say it is ultimately better to marry someone of your own race.[14] So, the picture is not totally grim, but there is room for improvement.

> **FACT**
> Interracial marriage was not legal in the United States until 1967, when the Supreme Court declared that a ban on interracial marriage was unconstitutional.

Dealing with Parents Who Can't Deal

If you are in an interracial relationship and your parents are not accepting of it, here are some things you can do to help your situation:

◉ Ask them why they do not feel that interracial dating is okay (do not ask them about your relationship in particular—instead, focus on the general). Ask this

MOVIE REVIEW
Jungle Fever (1991)
In this Spike Lee movie, Flipper (who's black) and Angie (white) meet when she is assigned to his firm as a temp. To Angie, Flipper is educated, successful, and the mythic black stud personified. To Flipper, Angie represents the beautiful white girls he always saw on television. Their relationship creates disapproval, causes violence, and makes everyone question whether two people of different races can ever love each other.

question in a serious tone and with respect so that you can understand their position.

◎ Explain your views on the issue. After you hear their side, calmly explain yours. Again, try not to get personal, but instead stay on a more general plane. Let them know that you have given a lot of thought to this issue and have your educated opinions.

◎ Talk about your friends of diverse backgrounds. Let your parents know that you associate with people of different colors, beliefs, and backgrounds.

◎ Maybe have your parents meet your partner. If your parents seem to open up to the idea of you dating someone of another race, or at least the idea that not everyone you associate with has to be like you, have your partner over for dinner. Make your parents see the wonderful person you have chosen to be with. Show them that the two of you respect and care for each other in a mature and responsible way.

DRINKING AND DRUGS AND SEX

Many people actually feel that they need to be "on something"—alcohol or another drug—in order to be able to have sex. True, in small quantities, alcohol lowers a person's inhibitions and gets them to relax. This, in turn, might make them feel more comfortable about being sexual. However, the effects of drinking and drugs on sexual performance and sexual safety are enormous. Consider the following:[15]

◎ Teens fourteen and younger who use alcohol are twice as likely to have sex than teens who do not drink. If these teens use drugs, they are four times more likely to have sex.

◎ Teens fifteen and older who drink are seven times more likely to have sex and twice as likely to have sex with four or more partners.

◎ Prolonged drinking of alcohol alters male sexual behavior. When males drink, the liver is stimulated and produces a substance that aids in the destruction of the male sex hormone. Also, excessive, prolonged drinking in males causes the withering away, or atrophy, of the testicles, enlargement of the breasts, and impotence (the ability to have an erection).

- People of any age, but especially teens, are less likely to use condoms (or use them properly if they do use them) while under the influence. No condom equals an increased chance in getting an STD or someone pregnant. In fact, one study found that almost half of all unplanned teen pregnancies happened as a result of sex under the influence of alcohol or drugs.[16]

- People who have sex with a person who is drunk can be convicted of rape. A person who is under the influence of drugs or alcohol loses her or his ability to consent to sex. Having sex with someone without their consent is rape.

- People do not think as clearly about things when they aren't sober. They may regret their actions of last night during the morning after. Friendships, relationships, and your self-respect can go down the tubes if you have sex when you are not thinking as clearly as you could be.

So, if having sex under the influence of either alcohol or drugs is so bad for you, why do so many people do it?

There is a lot of pressure out there to have sex. Some of this pressure comes from the media, some comes from your friends, and some of it comes from inside of you. There is a part of you that wants to have sex, but another part of you that knows that you should not. The reasons that you want to have sex might be curiosity, desire, to get props, or because it sounds like fun. The reasons you have for believing you should not have sex can range from "I do not believe sex before marriage is right," to "I just don't know this person well enough," to "It would be fun, but I already have a girl/boyfriend." So, you have this debate going on in your head about whether to have sex or not; what better way to end the debate than to eliminate one of the sides? By drinking or using drugs, the side that says you shouldn't have sex magically disappears. End of debate. The beginning of a whole lot of trouble.

Some of the reasons that so many people have sex while under the influence depend a lot on their gender. For girls, alcohol is a great excuse. Because girls who are sexually active, or who express sexual desire, are considered sluts (see chapter 8 for more thoughts on this), a girl may not want to simply say to another, or even herself, that she wants to have sex. But, if that girl gets drunk, she is no longer herself. Her flirting, desires, and other sexual advances can now be blamed on the alcohol instead of her personality; this girl is not really a slut, she is just drunk, or high, or whatever.

For guys, alcohol can be a great crutch to help them through a sexual encounter. Guys are supposed to want sex all the time. But, what if a guy knows that he should not be having sex, for whatever reason? As an intelligent person, this guy would choose not to have sex. But this guy also knows that a guy who does not want sex, or heaven forbid turns down a sexual proposition, is a total loser in the eyes of society and many teens (again, chapter 8 has a lot to say about this). Being under the influence of alcohol or another drug helps a guy feel as though he wants to have the sex he is "supposed" to have—losing sobriety helps a guy silence the common sense that contradicts all the social messages he is receiving so that it's easier to fit in. Also, being a little tipsy might help a guy take potential rejection a bit more easily.

The bottom line is that sex and alcohol or drugs is a typical, but dangerous combination. If you don't think you would be able to have sex without taking something first, think again about having sex.

Conclusion

14

When it comes to knowing all you need to know about sex and relationships, this book barely covers the tip of the iceberg. There's so much to know and every person has different needs for different information. However, I do hope this book helps you realize that you have already experienced a lot in your life and encourages you to keep learning about things that are important to you, or just plain interesting. Asking questions about sex can only make you wiser. Keep this book around for a reference, in case you forget some of the facts you read. You can always reread sections if you need a reminder. Recommend or pass this book along to a friend if you think there is someone out there you care about who could learn a thing or two from it.

My goals for writing this book were to help youth think about how they feel about different aspects of sex and relationships and encourage them to make responsible sexual decisions that reflect their feelings, values, and who they are. Ultimately, you're the one who will decide what you do and do not believe is right and what you do and do not want to do sexually. All this book can offer are facts, different perspectives, and suggestions to make your decisions more informed. Just remember—every decision you make about sex has its consequences, and all possible results are important to consider when making decisions about sex. However, if you're ever in a situation where you're forced to be sexual in any way against your will, you are not at fault. Talk to someone, get help right away. Your power to make a decision that's right for you is taken away under those circumstances and you shouldn't blame yourself for acting against your beliefs when you are forced to.

Paying attention to the feelings and wishes of others is a very nice thing to do in a relationship, but the bottom line is this—look after yourself first, do what is right for you, and in the long run you will be a much happier and healthier person.

Best of luck!

Notes

INTRODUCTION

1. See www.sacred-texts.com/sex/kama/kama101.htm (July 7, 2002).

CHAPTER 1

1. M. Warren and A. C. Petersen, *Girls at Puberty*, ed. J. Brooks-Gunn and A. C. Petersen (New York: Plenum Press, 1983).

2. R. C. Hayward, J. D. Killen, D. M. Wilson, L. D. Hammer, I. F. Litt, H. Kraemer, F. Haydel, A. Varady, and C. B. Taylor, "Psychiatric Risk Associated with Early Puberty in Adolescent Girls," *Journal of the American Academy of Child and Adolescent Psychiatry* 36, no. 2: 255–262, 1997.

3. Unless otherwise noted, all questions and answers are provided by the *We're Talking* teen health website. These questions were submitted by teens via their Web address, pamf.org/teen, and answered by doctors from the *We're Talking* website.

4. H. Finley, www.mum.org (July 7, 2002).

5. CNN news, "Menstruation and Sports," 2001, www.cnn.com/2000/HEALTH/mayo/09/08/menstruation.sports/ (May 22, 2002).

6. N. H. Alzubaidi, H. L. Chapin, V. H. Vanderhoof, K. A. Calis, and L. M. Nelson, "Meeting the Needs of Young Women with Secondary Amenorrhea and Spontaneous Premature Ovarian Failure," *Obstetrics & Gynecology* 99 (2002): 720–725.

7. Demelza Needham, Martine Carroll, Emileen Ng, Stine Braathen, "History of PMS in Western Society," *Premenstrual Syndrome*, 2001, remus.artsmmc.uwa.edu.au/www-projects/anth228328/meds/history.html (May 22, 2002).

8. S. A. Rathus, J. S. Nevid, and L. Fichner-Rathus, *Human Sexuality in a World of Diversity* (Boston, Mass.: Allyn and Bacon, 2002), 101–104.

CHAPTER 2

1. C. C. Freudenrich, "Male Sex Organs," How Stuff Works, www.howstuffworks.com/human-reproduction2.htm (June 2, 2002).

2. Rathus, Nevid, and Fichner-Rathus, 113.

3. Unless otherwise noted, all questions and answers are provided by the Palo Alto Medical Foundation. These questions were submitted by teens via their Web address, teenquestions@pamf.org, and answered by doctors from the Palo Alto Medical Foundation.

4. From L. K. Gowen's personal archives of questions and her responses.

5. J. Henkel, "Testicular Cancer: Survival High with Early Treatment," U.S.A. Food and Drug Administration 1996, www.fda.gov/fdac/features/196_test.html (June 4, 2002).

6. Erin Breitenbach, "Symptoms and Signs of Testicular Cancer," www.cancerlinksusa.com/testicular/symptoms.htm (June 4, 2002).

7. American Cancer Society, "What Are the Risk Factors for Testicular Cancer?" (American Cancer Society, 2001), www.cancer.org/eprise/main/docroot/CRI/content/CRI_2_4_2X_What_are_the_risk_factors_for_testicular_cancer_41?sitearea=PED (May 25, 2002).

8. L. Armstrong, "About Lance Armstrong" (Lance Armstrong Foundation, 2001), www.laf.org/About_Lance/ (March 13, 2002).

CHAPTER 3

1. UNICEF, *A League Table of Teenage Births in Rich Nations* (Florence, Italy: UN Children's Fund, 2001).

2. C. Gordon, S. Smith, and Jill P. Pell, "Teenage Pregnancy and Risk of Adverse Perinatal Outcomes Associated with First and Second Births: Population Based Retrospective Cohort Study," *British Medical Journal* 323 (2001): 476–479.

3. Alan Guttmacher Institute, *Teenagers' Sexual and Reproductive Health* (New York: Alan Guttmacher Institute, 2002) and SIECUS, *Fact Sheet: Teenage Pregnancy, Birth, and Abortion* (New York: SIECUS, 2002).

4. M. L. Doshi, "Accuracy of Consumer Performed In-Home Tests for Early Pregnancy Detection," *American Journal of Public Health* 76, no. 5 (1986): 512–514.

5. J. J. Lewis, "Abortion History" (About.com, 2002), womenshistory.about.com/library/weekly/aa012200.htm (July 22, 2002) and www.naral.org.

6. G. Benfield, "Pregnant Teens Face Difficult Decisions" (Children's Hospital Medical Center of Akron, 2002), www.akronchildrens.org/health-parenting/babybeat/old/pregteen.html (June 2, 2002).

7. M. Berry, "Risks and Benefits of Open Adoptions," *The Future of Children* 3, no. 1 (1993): 125–138.

8. C. Dennison, "The Role of Research in the Teenage Pregnancy Strategy for England," paper presented at the ninth biennial meeting of the Society for Research on Adolescence, New Orleans, Louisiana, April 2002.

9. Dennison, "The Role of Research."

CHAPTER 4

1. SIECUS, *Fact Sheet: Teenage Pregnancy, Birth, and Abortion* (New York: SIECUS, 2002).

2. Centers for Disease Control and Prevention, *Tracking the Hidden Epidemics: Trends in STDs in the United States* (Atlanta: Centers for Disease Control and Prevention, 2000), 2.

3. Unless otherwise noted, all questions and answers are provided by the Palo Alto Medical Foundation. These questions were submitted by teens via their Web address, teenquestions@pamf.org, and answered by doctors from the Palo Alto Medical Foundation.

4. STD Reference Centre of the South African Institute for Medical Research, "Chances of Acquiring an STD after One Episode of Intercourse with an Infected Person," as cited in J. MacKay, *The Penguin Atlas of Human Sexual Behavior* (New York: Penguin Group, 2000), 56.

5. T. Rosebury, *Microbes and Morals: The Strange Story of Venereal Disease* (New York: Ballentine Books, 1973).

6. Family Education Network, The Tuskeegee Syphilis Experiments, Infoplease.com, www.infoplease.com/ipa/A0762136.html (July 23, 2002).

7. U.S. Department of Health and Human Services, *Sexually Transmitted Disease Surveillance* 1999 (Atlanta: Centers for Disease Control and Prevention, September 2000), 8.

CHAPTER 5

1. SIECUS, *Teens Talk about Sex: Adolescent Sexuality in the 90's* (New York: SIECUS, 1994), 18.

2. SIECUS, *Teens Talk about Sex*, 24.

3. J. E. Darroch and S. Singh, *Why Is Teenage Pregnancy Declining? The Roles of Abstinence, Sexual Activity and Contraceptive Use* (New York: Alan Guttmacher Institute, 1999), 6.

4. L. M. Bogart, H. Cecil, D. A. Wagstaff, S. D. Pinkerton, and P. R. Abramson, "Is It Sex? College Students' Interpretations of Sexual Behavior Terminology," *Journal of Sex Research* 37, no. 2: 108–116, 2000.

5. R. Brasch, *How Did Sex Begin? The Sense and Nonsense of Sexual Customs and Traditions* (Australia: Angus and Roberts, 1995), 16–19.

6. This list was inspired, in part, by the work of Nathalie A. Bartle in her book *Venus in Blue Jeans* (New York: Houghton Mifflin Company, 1998).

7. Unless otherwise noted, all questions and answers are provided by the Palo Alto Medical Foundation. These questions were submitted by teens via their Web address, teenquestions@pamf.org, and answered by doctors from the Palo Alto Medical Foundation.

8. Messages reproduced by permission of Catie Gosselin, Webmaster of www.womanlinks.com.

CHAPTER 6

1. National Center for HIV, STD and TB Prevention, "HIV and Its Transmission" (Atlanta: Centers for Disease Control and Prevention, 2001), www.cdc.gov/hiv/pubs/facts/transmission.htm (February 23, 2002).

2. P. F. Horan, J. Phillips, and N. E. Hagan, "What Is Abstinence?" poster presented at the biennial meeting of the Society for Research in Child Development, Washington D.C., April 1997.

3. This concept was inspired by the work of Donnovan Somera and Carolyn Laub in their creation of an AIDS prevention program through the Mid-Peninsula YWCA in Mountain View, California.

4. This writing was inspired by earlier work I have done for courses on sex education for Stanford University and the Mid-Peninsula YWCA in Mountain View, California.

5. C. M. Grello and D. P. Welsh, "The Nature of Adolescents' Non-romantic Sexual Relationships and Their Link with Well-Being," poster presented at the ninth biennial meeting of the Society for Research on Adolescence, New Orleans, Louisiana, April 2002.

6. This concept was inspired by the work of Donnovan Somera and Carolyn Laub in their creation of an AIDS prevention program through the Mid-Peninsula YWCA in Mountain View, California.

7. J. H. Kellogg, *Plain Facts for Old and Young: Embracing the Natural History and Hygiene of Organic Life.* Made available by the University of Virginia Electronic Library, etext.lib.virginia.edu/etcbin/toccer-new2?id=KelPlai. sgm&images=images/modeng&data=/texts/english/modeng/ parsed&tag=public&part=9&division=div1 (February 14, 2002).

8. E. M. Duvall, *Facts of Life and Love for Teen-Agers* (Chicago: All Popular Library, 1957), 75.

CHAPTER 7

1. Office of the Assistant Secretary for Planning and Evaluation Trends in the Well-Being of America's Children and Youth 2000 (Washington, D.C.: U.S. Department of Health and Human Services, 2001).

2. C. S. Haignere, "Impact of Abstinence-until-Marriage Promises on Pregnancy," paper presented at the 130th annual meeting of the American Public Health Association, Philadelphia, Pa., November 2002.

3. Unless otherwise noted, all questions and answers are provided by the Palo Alto Medical Foundation. These questions were submitted by teens via their Web address, teenquestions@pamf.org, and answered by doctors from the Palo Alto Medical Foundation.

4. Adapted from a table by S. A. Rathus, J. S. Nevid, and L. Fichner-Rathus, *Human Sexuality in a World of Diversity* (Boston: Allyn and Bacon, 2002), 378–379.

CHAPTER 8

1. Many of the concepts in this chapter were inspired by the work of Donnovan Somera and Carolyn Laub in their creation of

an AIDS prevention program through the Mid-Peninsula YWCA in Mountain View, California.

2. L. Chunovic, *One Foot on the Floor: The Curious Evolution of Sex on Television from* I Love Lucy *to* South Park (New York: TV Books, 2000).

3. J. Peterson, K. Moore, and F. Furstenberg, "Television Viewing and Early Initiation of Sexual Intercourse: Is There a Link?" *Journal of Homosexuality* 21 (1991): 93–118.

4. D. Kunkel, K. Cope-Farrar, E. Biely, W. J. M. Farinola, and E. Donnerstein, *Sex on TV* (Santa Barbara, Calif.: Kaiser Family Foundation, 2001), 23.

5. Kunkel et al., *Sex on TV*, 36.

6. Kunkel et al., *Sex on TV*, 29.

7. Kunkel et al., *Sex on TV*, 36.

8. Unless otherwise noted, all questions and answers are provided by the Palo Alto Medical Foundation. These questions were submitted by teens via their Web address, teenquestions@pamf.org, and answered by doctors from the Palo Alto Medical Foundation.

9. This story was originally told by Carolyn Laub while teaching an AIDS prevention program through the Mid-Peninsula YWCA in Mountain View, California. Theresa is still alive, but ill, at the time of this writing.

10. Questions taken from the former AOL-based website ontheline.org.

CHAPTER 9

1. SIECUS, *Teens Talk about Sex: Adolescent Sexuality in the 90's* (New York: SIECUS, 1994), 47.

2. From L. K. Gowen's personal archives of online questions and her responses.

3. Unless otherwise noted, all questions and answers are provided by the Palo Alto Medical Foundation. These questions were submitted by teens via their Web address, teenquestions@pamf.org, and answered by doctors from the Palo Alto Medical Foundation.

CHAPTER 10

1. M. J. Zimmer-Gembeck, J. Siebenbruner, and W. A. Collins, "Diverse Aspects of Dating: Associations with

Psychosocial Functioning from Early to Middle Adolescence," *Journal of Adolescence* 24, no. 3 (June 2001).

2. J. G. Silverman, A. Raj, L. A. Mucci, and J. E. Hathaway, "Dating Violence against Adolescent Girls and Associated Substance Use, Unhealthy Weight Control, Sexual Risk Behavior, Pregnancy, and Suicidality," *JAMA* 286, no. 5 (2001): 575.

3. This story was first told by Donnovan Somera during an AIDS prevention program given by the Mid-Peninsula YWCA in Mountain View, California.

4. The question and answer were taken from my online archives of questions and answers.

5. *Webster's Dictionary*, "Jealousy," Dictionary.com 1998, www.dictionary.com/search?q=jealousy (April 22, 2002).

6. *Webster's Dictionary*, "Betrayal," Dictionary.com 1998, www.dictionary.com/search?q=betrayal (April 22, 2002).

CHAPTER 11

1. J. G. Silverman, A. Raj, L. A. Mucci, and J. E. Hathaway, "Dating Violence against Adolescent Girls and Associated Substance Use, Unhealthy Weight Control, Sexual Risk Behavior, Pregnancy, and Suicidality, *JAMA* 286, no. 5 (2001): 575.

2. V. I. Rickert and C. M. Wiemann, "Date Rape among Adolescents and Young Adults," *Journal of Pediatric and Adolescent Gynecology* 11, no. 4 (1998): 167–175.

3. The National Organization on Male Sexual Victimization, "Sexually Victimized Boys," NoMSV.org, http://161.58.139.13/articles/vcpn.html (June 5, 2002).

4. C. Schoen, K. Davis, C. DesRoches, and A. Shekhdar, "The Health of Adolescent Boys, Commonwealth Survey Findings," The Commonwealth Fund, www.cmwf.org/programs/women/boysv271.asp (July 22, 2002).

CHAPTER 12

1. C. M. Rennison, "Criminal Victimization 1998" (U.S. Department of Justice, 1998), www.rainn.org/test/cv98.pdf (February 3, 2002).

2. A. Coxell, M. King, G. Mezey, and D. Gordon, "General Practice: Lifetime Prevalence, Characteristics, and Associated Problems of Non-consensual Sex in Men: Cross-Sectional

Survey," *British Medical Journal* 318 (March 27, 1999): 846–850.

3. E. O. Laumann, J. H. Gagnon, R. T. Michael, and S. Michaels, *The Social Organization of Victimization: Sexual Practices in the United States* (Chicago: University of Chicago Press, 1994), 338.

4. Illinois Coalition Against Sexual Assault, *Acquaintance Rape: When the Rapist Is Someone You Know* (Illinois Coalition Against Sexual Assault, 1990), rivervision.com/safe/arwhat.html (June 24, 2002).

5. Unless otherwise noted, all questions and answers are provided by the Palo Alto Medical Foundation. These questions were submitted by teens via their Web address, teenquestions@pamf.org, and answered by doctors from the Palo Alto Medical Foundation.

6. National Center for Policy Analysis, "Crime and Punishment in America: Study #193," (National Center for Policy Analysis, 1998), www.ncpa.org/studies/s193/s193b.html (February 3, 2002).

7. Rape, Abuse, and Incest National Network, "RAINN Statistics," 2000, www.rainn.org/statistics.html (February 3, 2002).

CHAPTER 13

1. L. K. Gowen, C. Hayward, J. D. Killen, T. N. Robinson, and C. B. Taylor, "Acculturation and Eating Disorder Symptoms in Adolescent Girls," *Journal of Research on Adolescence* (1999): 67–84.

2. L. M. Irving, M. Wall, D. Neumark-Sztainer, and M. Story, "Steroid Use among Adolescents: Findings from Project EAT," *Journal of Adolescent Health* 30, no. 4 (2002): 243–252.

3. D. Neumark-Sztainer and P. J. Hannan, "Weight-Related Behaviors among Adolescent Girls and Boys: Results from a National Survey," *Archives of Pediatrics & Adolescent Medicine* 154 (2000): 569–577.

4. J. Polivy and C. P. Herman, "Diagnosis and Treatment of Normal Eating," *Journal of Consulting and Clinical Psychology* 55, no. 5 (1987): 635–644.

5. For a summary of this literature see L. K. Gowen, "Heterosociability and Weight Concerns in Early Adolescent Females," dissertation submitted to the Stanford University School of Education, 1998.

6. Facts taken from a review in L. K. Gowen and S. S. Feldman, "The Sexual Behaviors and Attitudes of Adolescent Girls with Older vs. Same-Aged Boyfriends," unpublished manuscript, Stanford Center on Adolescence, 2000.

7. Quotes taken from the personal archives of L. K. Gowen's message boards.

8. B. Summersgill, "Sodomy Laws," www.sodomylaws.org (July 22, 2002).

9. A. S. Walters and D. M. Hayes, "Homophobia within Schools: Challenging the Culturally Sanctioned Dismissal of Gay Students and Colleagues," *Journal of Homosexuality* 35, no. 2 (1998): 1–23.

10. C. Ryan and D. Futterman, "Lesbian and Gay Youth: Care and Counseling," *Adolescent Medicine: State of the Art Reviews* 8, no. 2 (1998).

11. K. S. Petersen, "Interracial Dating," *USA Today*, November 3, 1997, accessed at www.angelfire.com/super2/beme0/index.html (July 14, 2002).

12. Alloy, "The Interracial Dating Survey!" Alloy.com www.alloy.com/reallife/issuesandadvice/surveyresults/interracialdating/ (July 14, 2002).

13. Petersen, "Interracial Dating."

14. Kaiser Family Foundation, "Race and Ethnicity in 2001: Attitudes, Perceptions, and Experiences" (Kaiser Family Foundation, 2001), www.kff.org/content/2001/3143/RacialBiracialToplines.pdf (July 14, 2002).

15. McKinley Health Center, "What You Should Know about Sex and Alcohol but Were Afraid to Ask" (McKinley Health Center, University of Illinois, 2001), www.mckinley.uiuc.edu/health-info/drug-alc/sex-alco.html (January 22, 2002).

16. Cited in S. Foster, "Early Use of Booze, Drugs Leads to Sex and Problems," *San Diego Union-Tribune*, January 23, 2000.

For Further Information

Need more information? Check out these books, web-sites, and hot lines to get the facts you need to live a better, more educated life!

BOOKS

Bell, Ruth. *Changing Bodies, Changing Lives*. New York: Random House, 1998.
The book is so big because it has it all. Information not only on sex and sexuality, but also substance use, eating disorders, and your emotions. For both guys and gals.

Brumberg, J. J. *The Body Project: An Intimate History of American Girls*. New York: Vintage Books, 1997.
The history of feminine beauty from skin care to bras to tampons.

Columbia University's Health Education Program. *The Go Ask Alice Book of Answers*. New York: Henry Holt and Company, 1998.
If you are looking for an answer to a certain question, you have to use the index. But this book based on Columbia University's website, gives people great thorough answers to difficult sex and health questions.

D'Emilio, J., and E. B. Freedman. *Intimate Matters: A History of Sexuality in America*. New York: Harper and Row, 1988.
A bit dense, but a great historical perspective on the history of sex in America.

Drill, E., H. McDonald, and R. Odes. *Deal with It*. New York: Simon and Schuster, 1999.

Written for girls, but with information boys may find interesting. Lots of neat quotes to let you know that you are not the only one thinking those weird thoughts.

Due, L. *Joining the Tribe: Growing Up Gay and Lesbian in the '90s*. New York: Anchor Books, 1995.
Stories by young adults who don't consider themselves heterosexual. They talk about high school, college, the bar scene, and life in general.

Lopez, R. I. *The Teen Health Book: A Parent's Guide to Adolescent Health and Well-Being*. New York: W. W. Norton and Company, 2002.
Sure, it is written for parents, but this book, written by a doctor, has all the health facts you need written in pretty clear language.

Rue, N. *Coping with Dating Violence*. New York: Rosen Publishing Group, 1989.
A bit old, but not outdated. Talks about abuse from both the boys' side and the girls' side.

Vitkus, J. *Smart Sex*. New York: Simon and Schuster, 1998.
Put out by the folks of MTV, it is a fun read with a lot of facts, but may not give you all the information you need. Great celebrity interviews.

Williams, D. M. *Sensual Celibacy*. New York: Simon and Schuster, 1999.
Reminds you of all the great things you could be doing for yourself and your self-esteem if you weren't so wrapped up in sex.

WEBSITES

I Wanna Know www.iwannaknow.org
Information galore about sexual health.

The Alan Guttmacher Institute www.agi-usa.org
Heavy on the research, this organization is great for school research or to get the most reliable information.

Birth Mother www.birthmother.com
An unbiased site for mothers- and fathers-to-be considering
adoption.

Get the Facts www.getthefacts.org
Learn about all the politics surrounding sex education in
schools. Information, articles, and up-to-date information
on the latest Congress debates!

Go Ask Alice www.goaskalice.columbia.edu/
This site is very popular, so you may not get your question
answered, but there are so many archives (searchable!),
chances are, someone has already asked. Check it out!

The Sexuality Information and Education Council of the
United States www.siecus.org.
A nonprofit whose goal is for everyone to have access to
accurate information on sex and sexual health. Great
section for teens, but also a place for political activists and
educators.

Youth Action Online www.youth.org
A great site for gay and bi teens, or those who just want to
learn more about sexual orientation.

We're Talking teen health website www.pamf.org/teen
Provides great health information for teens, as well as a link
to a place you can ask any health question and a doctor
will answer it.

Parents and Friends of Gays and Lesbians www.pflag.org
A great national organization that supports gay teens and
those who care about them.

Safer Sex www.safersex.org
All you ever wanted to know about what is and isn't safe.

Sex Etc. www.sxetc.org
A newsletter written by older teens about sex and sexuality.
Put out by Rutgers University.

Teen Wire www.teenwire.com
Planned Parenthood's site for teens. Lots of information,
plus a directory of where to find the nearest Planned
Parenthood clinic.

True Love Waits http://www.lifeway.com/tlw/
The campaign that challenges teenagers and college
students to remain sexually abstinent until marriage.

RAINN www.rainn.org
A celebrity-supported site on sexual abuse and rape.
Accurate information along with a list of places to get help
and support.

HOT LINES

Need someone to talk to? Check out these toll-free lines
and call someone who knows what's going on. They are
there because they want to help YOU.

ORGANIZATION	PHONE NUMBER
Boston Alliance for Gay and Lesbian Youth	1-800-42BAGLY
Boys Town National Hotline Dial up to talk about anything getting you down	1-800-448-3000
Child Help USA If you believe you live in an abusive home, give these people a call	1-800-422-4453
Covenant House Nineline For runaways	1-800-999-9999
National Domestic Violence Hotline	1-800-799-7233 (SAFE)
National AIDS Hotline	1-800-342-AIDS
Spanish	1-800-344-7432
TTY	1-800-243-7889

National STD Hotline   1-800-227-8922

Planned Parenthood   1-800-230-PLAN (7526)
    Find the clinic nearest you

RAINN   1-800-656-HOPE
    This hot line will
    automatically transfer
    you to the rape crisis
    center nearest you,
    anywhere in the nation

Suicide Hotlines   1-800-784-2433
    This hot line will help you
    find the nearest suicide
    hot line to you

Teens and AIDS Hotline   1-800-234-TEEN

Index

abortion, 32–34; history of,
32–33; types of, 34–35
abortion pill. *See* RU-486
abstinence, 65, 75–78, 97–98
abuse, emotional, 165
abuse, family, 168
abuse, physical, 165
abuse, sexual, 165–66
abusive relationships, 163–67,
169; getting out of, 167–69;
recovery from, 169
adoption, 36–39; confidential,
37; open, 37
AIDS. *See* HIV/AIDS
alcohol, 201–3
amenorrhea, 9–10
Armstrong, Lance, 24

babies, 43
baby blues, 44
betrayal, 159–60
bimanual examination, 12
birth control, 93; barrier
methods of, 99; chance,
94–95; effectiveness rates,
119; hormonal methods,
111; a withdrawal, 95. *See
also* specific methods of
birth control
blood test, 57–58, 85
body image, 181–83
bondage, 189
breaking up, 192–93

breast examination, 12
breasts, 1, 14–15

cancer: cervical, 51–52; penis,
51; testicular, 22, 24;
vaginal, 51
casual sex, 82–83
cervical cap, 108–9
chancres, 54
cheating, 159–60
cherry. *See* hymen
chlamydia, 48, 57, 59
circumcision, 19–20, 22
clinic, 84
clitoris, 1, 12–14
cold sores, 51. *See also* Herpes
simple Type I (cold sores)
coming out, 197–98
communication, 139–42,
144–45, 157
compromise, 156–57
condoms, 99–108; breakage of,
104–5; putting on, 101–3;
types of, 103–8
conflict, in relationships,
160–61
consent, 172–73
contraception. *See* birth
control, *see also* specific
methods of birth control
cramps, 11
crushes, 152–55
cum. *See* semen

dating, 150–52, 183–85
dating violence, 163–64, 166
Depo-Provera, 114–16
diaphragm, 108–9
discharge, 1, 7–8
doctor, 58–59, 84
drinking. *See* alcohol
drugs, 202–3

eating disorders, 2, 181–83
egg. *See* ovum
ejaculation, 18, 25–26
Elders, Dr. Jocelyn, 91
emergency contraception. *See* morning-after pill
endometrium, 5
epdidymis, 18, 23
erection, 18–20
estrogen, 5–6
ethnicity, 62, 133–34

fallopian tubes, 4
fat, body, 13
female ejaculation, 13
fetishes, 187
foreskin, 19–20, 22

G-spot, 14
genital warts. *See* HPV (human papilloma virus)
GHB (gamma hydroxy butyrate), 174–75
gonorrhea, 49, 56
growth spurt, 1, 17
gynecologist, 11–12

Hepatitis B, 50
Herpes simplex type I (cold sores), 51
Herpes simplex type II (genital herpes), 50
HIV/AIDS, 53

homophobia, 196, 199
hormones, 5, 188. *See also* estrogen, progesterone, testosterone
HPV (human papilloma virus), 51–52
hymen, 2–3, 71

interracial dating, 199–201
intimacy, 79–82
IUD (intra-uterine device), 111–12

jealousy, 158–59

Kama Sutra, xii
kissing, 51, 61

labels, 129–34, 136
labia, 1
labor and delivery, 42–43
lubricant, 22, 71, 100–102

masturbation, 13, 21, 87–90; history of, 90
media, 79, 125–28
menstrual cycle, 1, 4–8, 10, 27; irregular, 8; missed periods, 29
mixed messages, 143
monogamy, 83
morning-after pill, 120
morning sickness, 39
music, 131

name-calling. *See* labels
natural family planning (NFP), 95–96
nipples, 15

older guys, 183–85
online relationships, 189–92

orgasm: faking, 72; female, 13; male, 25

osteoporosis, 10

ovaries, 1, 4–5

ovulation, 6–7, 27

ovum, 4–6, 27

parental consent, 32–34

parents, xi–xii, 32–33, 146–48, 200–201

the "patch," 116–17

pelvic examination, 12

pelvic inflammatory disease (PID), 48–49, 112

penis, 17–21

penis size, 19

period. *See* menstrual cycle

Pill, birth control, 9, 112–14

Planned Parenthood, 32, 113

PMS (premenstrual syndrome), 10–11

pornography, 185–87

post-partum depression, 44

power, 25

pre-ejaculate, 25, 95

pregnancy, 27–29, 31, 39; tests, 29–31, 114; signs of, 29; stages of, 40–43

pressure: gender, 129–36; partner, 124–25; peer, 121–24

progesterone, 6, 111

puberty, 2, 18; female, 1; male, 17

pubic hair, 1, 17

pubic lice, 54

racial groups. *See* ethnicity

rape, 171–73, 176–78; acquaintance/date, 171; drugs, 174–75; examination, 176–77; prevention,

178–79; reporting, 177–78; resources/support, 175, 179–80; statistics, 173–74; statutory, 172; stranger, 171

refractory period, 25

relationships, 79, 81, 140, 149–52, 155, 157–58, 184

respect, 156

the "ring," 116–17

Rohypnol, 174–75

roofies. *See* Rohypnol

RU-486, 35–36

safer sex, 75, 87, 121, 134–35

Sanger, Margaret, 113

scabies, 54

schools, xi

scrotum, 17

self-examination, female, 14

semen, 17–18

sex, 61–62; choosing not to have, 75, 77–78, 97–98; education, xi–xiii; decision-making about, 62–64, 67–68, 123, 204; definition of, 64–66, 76; first time, 68–72,

sexual behavior, 78–81

sexual orientation, 195–99

sexually-transmitted diseases. *See* STDs

sharing, 188

smoking, 113

speculum, 12

sperm, 18, 27–28

spermicide, 107, 108–11, 119

sports, 9–10

spotting, 9

STDs, 25, 45–49, 52–56, 59, 76–77; bacterial, 47; critters, 47; prevention of, 93;

symptoms of, 56–57; testing for, 57–58, 83–85; types of, 47, 50; viral, 47. *See also* specific STDs
stereotypes, 133–37
sterilization: female, 118. *See also* tubal ligation; male, 117. *See also* vasectomy
swab test, 57–58, 85
sweat glands, 17
syphilis, 54–55

tampons, 2–3, 7
teen pregnancy, 28–30, 43, 64
television, 125–28
testicles, 17–18, 22–23, 26
testicular cancer. *See* cancer, testicular
testicular self-examination (TSE), 22–23

testosterone, 17, 21
threesomes, 188
trichomoniasis, 55
trust, 155–56, 159
tubal ligation, 118–19
tubal pregnancy, 48–49
turn-ons, 187
Tuskegee experiments, 55

urine test, 57–58,
uterus, 1, 4, 6

vagina, 1–3
vas deferens, 18
vasectomy, 117–18
virginity, 2, 64–66, 68; losing, 69–73

wet dream, 17
withdrawal, 95

About the Author

Kris received her Ph.D. in child and adolescent development from Stanford School of Education in 1998, and her Ed.M. in human development and psychology from the Harvard Graduate School of Education in 1994. Since then, she has published several professional articles on adolescent health with foci on sex education and body image. Her advice on teen health has appeared in *Teen People, Young and Modern* (where she served on the advisory board), and on several websites.

Kris currently teaches human sexuality and women's health at Portland State University. She lives in Portland, Oregon, and is an avid hockey fan.